The UK Economy
2005-2015

Nick Fyfe
Head of Economics, Dulwich College

Andrew Threadgould
Staff Tutor, Dulwich College

Acknowledgements and thanks

Many thanks to Peter Maunder for all his efforts and expertise as editor and advisor,
to Ian Black for his work on previous editions, and to Martin Stanley for his
specific and up to date expertise on competition policy.

Anforme Ltd, Stocksfield Hall, Stocksfield, Northumberland NE43 7TN.

Typeset by George Wishart & Associates, Whitley Bay.
Printed by Potts Print (UK) Ltd.

Contents

	Introduction	iv
Chapter 1	**GDP: Boom, Bust and Recovery**	1
Chapter 2	**Consumer Spending, Saving and Credit**	11
Chapter 3	**UK plc: Business and Industry**	21
Chapter 4	**Living Standards, Poverty and Inequality**	30
Chapter 5	**UK Trade, the Current Account and the Value of the Pound**	47
Chapter 6	**The Supply Side: Productivity and Competitiveness**	55
Chapter 7	**Employment and Unemployment**	63
Chapter 8	**Inflation and Deflation**	73
Chapter 9	**Monetary Policy in the UK**	82
Chapter 10	**UK Fiscal Policy**	91
Chapter 11	**The United Kingdom and Europe**	102
Chapter 12	**The UK in the World Economy**	110
	Index	Inside Back Cover

Chapter 1

GDP: Boom, Bust and Recovery

Introduction

The story of UK GDP growth between 2005 and 2015 is complex. The NICE decade of non-inflationary continuous expansion ended with the credit crisis of 2007 and was followed by the recession of 2008-09. In the years since, the UK economy has returned to growth with output rising and unemployment falling alongside low inflation.

● Knowledge: Economic growth

Economic growth – the increase in the productive capacity in an economy – is a fundamental measure of macroeconomic performance. The trend rate of economic growth for the UK economy has been assumed for several years to be between 2.5% and 2.75% per year. This implies that the total output of the economy, if all factors of production (land, labour, capital, enterprise) were fully utilised, would grow by this percentage each year.

However measuring productive capacity is very difficult, and thus economists focus on the more accessible measure of economic growth as the percentage change in Gross Domestic Product (GDP). GDP measures actual output: the total value of output in the whole economy over a given period of time.

● Application: A brief history of UK growth

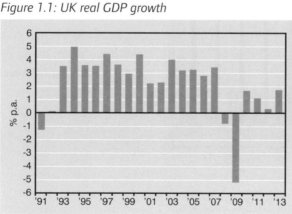

Figure 1.1: UK real GDP growth

Source: HM Treasury

As Figure 1.1 shows, the actual growth rate of the UK economy has fluctuated significantly from year to year.

A **recession** occurs where real GDP growth is negative for at least two consecutive quarters. Over the period shown in Figure 1.1 the UK economy experienced two recessions: in the early 1990s and in 2008-09. In addition, the UK economy was initially believed to have re-entered recession in late 2011 and early 2012 but later revisions of the data showed this was narrowly avoided. A **boom** is a period during which real GDP rises at a faster rate than assumed growth in productive capacity. The long boom of 1997-2007 can clearly be seen on Figure 1.1.

Recovery, or upturn, often marks the period between the end of a recession and the beginning of a boom. During this stage of the economic cycle, real GDP is positive, rising, but still below the long-run growth rate. On the other hand, a slowdown or downturn occurs when real GDP growth is positive but falling and is below the long-run growth rate.

Question

1. Using Figure 1.1, give examples of each of the following: boom, slowdown, recession, recovery.

Macroeconomic policies tend to focus on creating stable and sustainable economic growth. **Supply-side policies** aim to increase the long-run average, or trend level of growth which shows increases in productive capacity. This will be explored in greater detail in Chapter 6 when we examine productivity and competitiveness in greater detail. **Demand-management policies** such as fiscal and monetary measures are used to control actual GDP and take a shorter-term approach to macroeconomic stability. These policies are explored in greater depth in Chapters 9 and 10 respectively.

When investigating the story of the UK in recent years, economic growth is a key indicator of the health and potential of the UK macroeconomy.

● ● Application **and Analysis: Components of UK GDP**

GDP measures the total value of output, expenditure and incomes across the economy over a given period of time. Macroeconomists break down GDP into four key areas:

Consumption (C)   Spending by households on consumer goods e.g. food, holidays, clothes

Investment (I)   Spending by firms on capital goods e.g. machinery, vehicles, plant

Government Spending (G)   Spending by the public sector e.g. infrastructure, public sector wages, NHS costs

Net Exports (X-M)   Spending by foreigners on UK goods minus spending by the UK on foreign goods

Figure 1.2: UK GDP by component

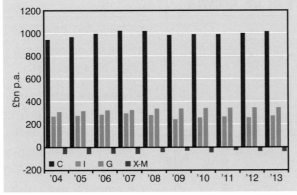

Source: HM Treasury

Figure 1.2 shows the importance of consumer spending for the UK economy over the period shown. The effect of the recession in 2008-09 can be seen on both consumption and investment, along with the fall in net exports resulting from recession in the UK's main trading partners.

Figure 1.3: Economic growth in the UK by component

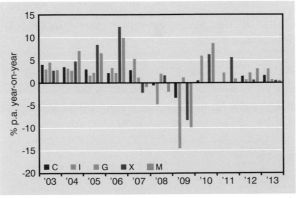

Source: HM Treasury

Figure 1.3 shows how each of these components changed over the same period.

● Analysis: **Explaining fluctuations in real GDP growth**

Figure 1.4: UK business confidence in the service and manufacturing sector

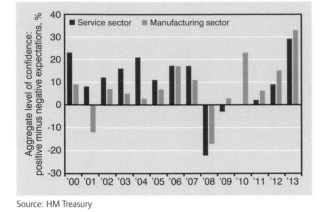

Source: HM Treasury

Figure 1.5: UK consumer confidence

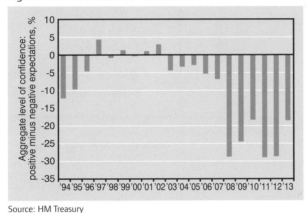

Source: HM Treasury

1991-1997: Recession and export-led growth

The UK experienced recession in the early 1990s. Stock markets crashed in 1987 in the USA and across Europe. The UK economy continued to grow until 1990 but as oil prices were pushed higher by the Gulf War, both consumer price inflation and the base rate reached double figures. Falling real incomes and the negative wealth effect from a struggling housing market pushed the UK into its deepest recession since the Second World War. In September 1992 the domestic currency, sterling, was forced out of the Exchange Rate Mechanism, which was the system used to ensure national currencies converged in preparation for the creation of the single European currency, the euro.

The period 1992-97 saw recovery from recession. The weaker value of sterling helped to boost exports, particularly to other European countries, and although business and consumer confidence was not always high – see Figure 1.5 – and the housing market was flat over this period, for example there were signs of growth in the service sector and the UK economy began to emerge as a modern, service-based consumer economy.

Spending by households on consumer goods such as clothes is the most important element of UK GDP.

Figure 1.6: UK base rate of interest

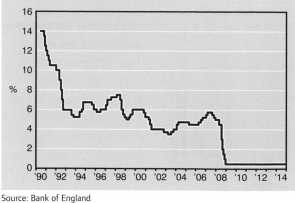

Source: Bank of England

Figure 1.7: UK unemployment

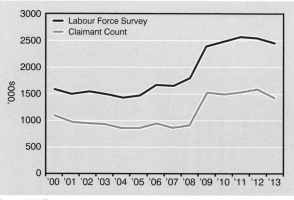

Source: HM Treasury

Figure 1.8: Long-term and youth unemployment in the UK

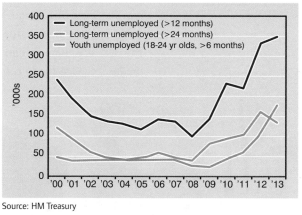

Source: HM Treasury

Figure 1.9: UK inflation, Consumer Price Index

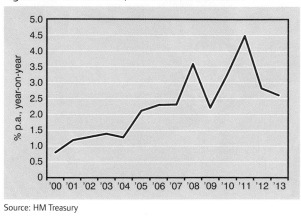

Source: HM Treasury

1997-2000: Early days of New Labour

With a New Labour government in place with an emphasis on growth and economic stability, the UK economy began a period of significant expansion. The control of monetary policy and the setting of interest rates was handed to the newly-independent Bank of England, and although the new administration pledged to maintain Conservative spending plans for their first three years in power, the intention of significant public sector investment in education and healthcare was clear.

The 'feel good factor' returned to the UK economy:

- interest rates fell through 1998 and 1999 (from 7.25% in May 1998 to 5% by June 1999; figures for 1990-2014 are shown on Figure 1.6)

- unemployment continued to fall, in particular long-term and youth unemployment

- low and falling inflationary pressure

- the housing market experienced its strongest growth since the early 1990s, increasing household wealth through positive equity for homeowners (Figure 1.10)

- strong stock market performance, increasing household wealth for shareholders (Figure 1.11)

These factors combined to boost consumption and investment, and confidence also grew in expectation of an extensive programme of public sector investment.

Figure 1.10: UK housing market indicators

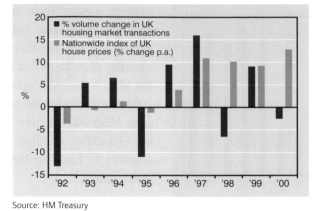

Source: HM Treasury

Figure 1.11: FTSE All Share Index, annual average

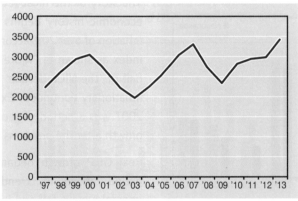

Source: HM Treasury

Figure 1.12: NASDAQ Composite Index, annual average

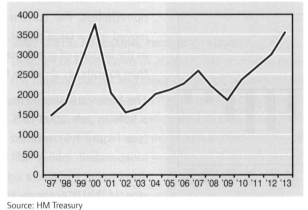

Source: HM Treasury

Figure 1.13: Annual change in selected stock market indices

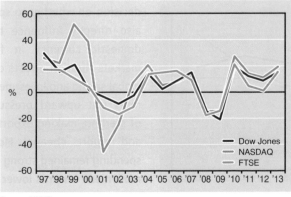

Source: HM Treasury

2000-2003: Turbulent times

By the turn of the millennium, it was clear the 'mini-boom' of 1997-2000 was coming to an end. The FTSE index increased by less than 5% over 2000 compared to double-digit growth in 1996-99 (see Figure 1.11). Even before the terrorist attacks in New York in September 2001, the US economy had faltered as the dot-com boom (and associated economic expansion created by the growth of new technology spending and investment) came to an end.

On March 10, 2000 the NASDAQ (the second-largest stock exchange in the USA, which pioneered online trading and was the exchange of choice for the new technology firms associated with the internet boom of 1995-2000) Composite index reached its peak of 5,132.52. Figure 1.12 shows the average annual values of this index between 1995 and 2013.

Over the course of 2001, the NASDAQ lost almost half of its value, with significant losses also recorded on the Dow Jones and FTSE indices (Figure 1.13).

These problems in the US economy were compounded by the tragic events in New York on the 9th September 2001, and the economic impact in the UK was one of shaken confidence and fears for future growth. The saving ratio for UK households, which had fallen steadily since the early 1990s recorded a small increase in 2001 (see Figure 1.14), and house price growth dipped in 2000 and 2001, albeit still increasing above the rate of inflation (housing market transactions also continued to rise as shown in Figure 1.15).

● Analysis: **Causes of the UK recession, 2008-2009**

The economic conditions of 2007-09 are regarded by some economists as a 'perfect storm': a combination of factors which combined to drive the economy into recession. These factors are:

● a financial crisis which increased the costs of borrowing for firms and households as banks feared collapse due to their exposure to bad debts

● a subsequent tightening of access to finance for both households and firms

● falling house prices (especially in the USA), exposing mortgage lenders to serious losses and reducing consumer confidence and household wealth

● significant losses on stock markets

● high levels of household debt due to cheap, easy finance and a falling saving ratio in the NICE decade

● rising oil prices (an increase from $55 to $147 barrel between early 2007 and July 2008)

As aggregate demand (total spending in the economy; the sum of consumption, investment, government expenditure and net exports) fell, further problems were created.

● Analysis: **Impacts of the UK recession, 2008-2009**

● rising joblessness, particularly for long-term and youth unemployment

● fewer job vacancies as firms avoided recruitment due to uncertainty about the future

● falling living standards as average earnings fell (impact of higher unemployment bringing average earnings down, as well as pay freezes and below-inflation pay awards for those people still in work)

● higher demand for higher education places as school-leavers (and graduates pursuing postgraduate courses) sought to remain in education

● a fall in inflation on the RPI measure (Figure 1.21); the differences between CPI and RPI and therefore the explanation for the significant disparity between these measures in 2009 are given in Chapter 8

● a depreciation in sterling (see Chapter 5)

● pressure on the government's budget position, as tax revenues fell (due to downward pressure on incomes, spending and wealth) and spending increased (due to the automatic stabiliser of more unemployment benefit claimants)

Figure 1.21: RPI and CPI in UK

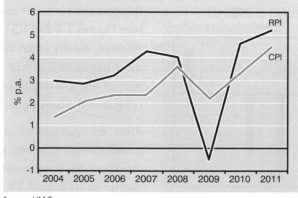

Source: HM Treasury

● Analysis: **Anti-recession policies**

The key policy instruments available to governments to control the level of aggregate demand in the economy are monetary and fiscal measures.

Monetary policy (This is discussed in detail in Chapter 9):

● drastic cuts in the base rate of interest (see Figure 1.6) culminating in a historically unprecedented base rate of 0.50% from March 2009

● a programme of quantitative easing beginning in March 2009: the purchase of government debt by the Bank of England (by February 2012, the Bank had authorised purchases of up to £325 bn)

● acceptance of a fall in the value of sterling, reducing the price of UK goods in international markets and stimulating export performance

Fiscal policy (This is discussed in detail in Chapter 10):

● cuts in tax rates, such as the temporary reduction in VAT from 17.5% to 15% in December 2008

● increases in other taxes, such as the introduction of a top rate of income tax of 50% on earnings over £150,000 per annum and a reduction of tax relief on pensions for high earners

● higher government spending on initiatives such as an extra £1.7bn on the job centre network, to support job seekers, and to help businesses during difficult trading conditions

● the scope for fiscal expansion has been limited due to the Coalition government's focus on closing the budget deficit ('austerity' policies) rather than to stimulate GDP growth to trigger automatic stabilisers

Question

3. Which policies are likely to be most effective in reducing the severity of a recession?

● Evaluation: **Economic recovery and future prospects?**

Figure 1.22: UK GDP, quarter-on-quarter growth (%)

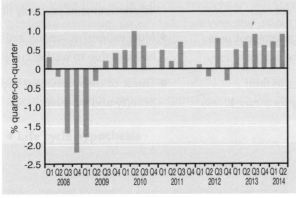

Source: HM Treasury

Figure 1.22 shows the quarterly growth data for the UK economy.

UK GDP returned to its pre-crisis level in Q2 of 2014 as the economy grew at an annualised rate of 3.1%. Relevant economic indicators will be explored in the chapters ahead, but most economists agree the headline picture is promising with the UK outpacing most other European economies into 2015.

There are several arguments explaining the story of GDP growth since 2009, including:

● Austerity measures have boosted confidence and innovation in the private sector of the economy, creating a 'crowding-in' dynamic and sustainable job creation and output.

● Austerity has slowed down the recovery: fiscal stimulus, rather than fiscal contraction, would have returned the economy to growth more quickly, reducing unemployment (and associated benefits) and generating tax revenue earlier.

- Loss of confidence in traditional pension schemes.

- Higher yields from other forms of 'saving', such as the buy-to-let market during the housing boom in the second half of the NICE decade.

- Lower interest rates for savers, especially since the drastic cuts in the base rate in 2009.

European countries where a 'pensions timebomb' are predicted to take place during the 21st century include the UK, Italy and Spain. A combination of high youth unemployment, high housing costs and a shift in culture away from 'traditional' family values may leave the economy short of workers (and therefore tax-payers) at a time when the cost of supporting an ageing population rises dramatically, given improvements in healthcare and rising life expectancies.

Figure 2.10 shows that, for the UK, the number of births has actually been rising since 2001. Some of this is due to greater immigration and higher birth rates in migrant families.

Policies which could be used to tackle the pensions timebomb problem include:

- Higher state pension retirement age (the age at which a state pension can be collected).

- Means-tested state pension (higher income households – typically those with significant private pensions – will no longer receive state pensions).

- Less generous state pension payments in real terms.

- Greater incentives to save for a pension, e.g. higher tax relief on employee and employer contributions.

- Extensive public information campaigns to alert young workers to the importance of preparing for retirement.

- Greater labour market flexibility to allow older workers to remain working, perhaps in part-time or flexible capacities.

- Compulsory employer pension contributions.

- A minimum retirement age for private as well as state pension funds.

- A 'laissez-faire' approach, where older workers who have not saved sufficiently will have no choice but to continue working or depend on other benefits, e.g. disability or sickness payments.

- Compulsory individual pension tax (this has been introduced in Australia).

The pension issue is a very good example of how long-term problems which require long-term solutions are often ignored by governments of the day. **Public choice theory** suggests that governments do not, in reality, aim to maximise social welfare, but rather seek re-election by 'buying' votes with policies which appeal to their core electorate. The likely popularity of the policies listed above offers an insight into the likelihood of core reforms taking place before more drastic decisions have to be made.

One important point to consider is whether these projected increases in life expectancy will actually occur. Highly developed societies may actually see health outcomes worsen due to factors such as stress, sedentary lifestyles, and high-fat diets. However, the worse case scenario for the public finances would be an increase in healthcare costs for the obese and unhealthy, but a continued rise in life expectancy: people could stay sicker for longer while unable to work, with drastic negative impacts on NHS and care costs.

Question Extension

5. The Australian government introduced a compulsory 'pension tax' in the 1990s.

   Evaluate the case for and against such a policy in the UK.

Chapter 3

Business and Industry

● ● Knowledge and Application: The structure of the UK economy

The term **economic growth** refers to increases in the productive capacity of an economy: how increases in the quantity and quality of factors of production can lead to higher output levels and a rising standard of living.

Over the past 300 years, the structure of the UK economy has undergone radical change. Modern economies such as the UK have typically experienced a series of 'revolutions' during which the dominant industries for employment and output have changed dramatically.

1. Industrial revolution

As new technologies in the *primary sector* (agricultural and energy extraction industries) developed, this liberated some land, labour and capital for use in the emerging *secondary sector* (manufacturing). Large numbers of households moved from the countryside to towns and cities to work in factories and mills. Thus **industrialisation** occurred alongside **urbanisation** and the manufacturing sector grew in importance throughout the 19th and 20th centuries. In terms of the agricultural sector, by 2012 60% of the UK's food needs were produced domestically by less than 2% of the workforce.

2. Post-industrial revolution

By the 1970s and 1980s, it was clear that the UK manufacturing sector was facing increasing competition from the resurgent economies of Germany and Japan, other trading partners within the expanding European Economic Community (the precursor to today's European Union) and from newly-industrialising countries such as Taiwan. The process of **deindustrialisation** saw British manufacturing face serious decline, as either UK-based firms moved production overseas, were driven out of business, or were absorbed into multinational conglomerates through merger or takeover.

Between 1997 and 2007, manufacturing output in the UK fell from 28% to 12% of GDP and manufacturing employment fell from one in four workers to one in ten. These changes were almost perfectly matched by an equivalent growth in service sector output and employment. However, as of 2009 the manufacturing sector employed 2.6 million British workers and the UK remained the world's sixth largest exporter by value of output, and a major exporter of technology-intensive manufactures. By 2000 the main threat to the UK's competitiveness in global manufacturing markets was the rapidly developing economies of China and India.

Figure 3.1: Growth in industrial production, selected economies

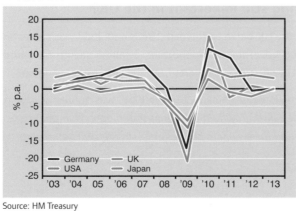

Source: HM Treasury

Figure 3.1 shows how UK industrial production growth compares with other regions and countries in recent years.

Clearly, all four of the economies shown in Figure 3.1 saw manufacturing output fall during the recession of 2008-09. The UK saw the lowest fall in output of those economies shown, but throughout the pre-recession period of 2001-07 the UK had the lowest average rate of growth (a contraction of 0.4%, compared with growth in the USA of 1.2%, 1.3% in Japan and 2.8% in Germany).

Figure 3.2: Growth in industrial production, UK, compared with the G7 average

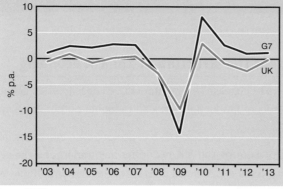

Source: HM Treasury

Figure 3.2 compares UK industrial growth with the G7 average. (The G7 group of countries comprises Canada, France, Germany, Italy, Japan, the USA and the UK.) Figure 3.2 shows that except for 2009, the G7 average growth rate outstripped growth in the UK economy.

● Analysis: Why has the UK experienced deindustrialisation?

Reasons for the decline in the importance of UK manufacturing within the UK and in global markets include:

- Loss of competitive advantage against lower-cost producers, including **newly-industrialising countries** (**NIC**s) such as China, Taiwan, South Korea and Singapore.

- Loss of competitive advantage against other advanced economies. As Figure 3.3 shows, the UK's labour costs grew faster than the G7 average throughout the period, even in 2010 when the G7 level fell.

Figure 3.3: UK and G7 unit labour costs in manufacturing

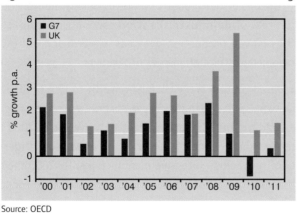

Source: OECD

- Increasingly globalised markets for traded goods which reduced transport costs to facilitate greater world trade.

- Relatively high land costs in the UK (linked to higher population density in urban areas).

- Relatively high labour costs in the UK (strong trade union power until the 1980s, and a higher standard of living and therefore higher cost of living).

- Weak investment in infrastructure, reducing the efficiency of national and international trading links.

● Evaluation: Is manufacturing still important in the UK?

The period of strong growth in the UK between the mid-1990s and 2007 was characterised by high levels of consumer demand, increased government expenditure, a falling saving ratio and a widening trade imbalance, as imports into the UK outstripped exports from the UK at a growing rate.

In May 2011, the Governor of the Bank of England, Mervyn King, was quoted as saying, *"The rebalancing of the UK economy which implies slow growth in consumer spending and in public spending will take not just one year but several years, and the switch to business investment and net exports will also take several years."*[1]

---

1. http://www.bbc.co.uk/blogs/thereporters/stephanieflanders/2011/05/inflation_up_growth_down_uncer.html

In common with many mature economies, the UK has experienced an expanding tertiary (service) sector as the secondary (manufacturing) sector has shrunk. This section will explore the key question: is the decline of manufacturing important?

The relevant factors to consider in answering this question include the following:

● Manufactured goods are easier to export than (most) services. The UK enjoys a strong position as a major provider of financial services such as banking and insurance and is also a major tourism destination (ranked sixth in the world) but other services are produced for predominantly domestic consumption, such as transport, healthcare and retail.

● Chapter 5, which examines the current account of the balance of payments, offers more detail regarding the balance of internationally traded goods and services. Trade in services has been in surplus (exports from the UK have exceeded imports into the UK) over every one of the past 20 years, whereas the trade in goods has been in deficit. It is important to note that the services surplus has been smaller than the goods deficit – a major contributor to the current account deficit in recent years.

● A shrinking manufacturing sector can also explain a relative decline in UK productivity. Technological innovation can increase productivity, usually by allowing labour (which can be expensive in a country such as the UK, where the cost of living is high) for cheaper capital (which, in the present century, can increasingly be produced in low-wage, low-rent NICs). Such substitution, however, is more difficult in the service sector industries where the UK enjoys a competitive advantage, such as tourism or financial services. Figure 3.4 shows how, despite the impact of recession on the data for 2009, manufacturing productivity growth has outstripped service sector productivity growth in recent years.

Figure 3.4: Productivity in UK manufacturing and service sectors (index, 2006 = 100)

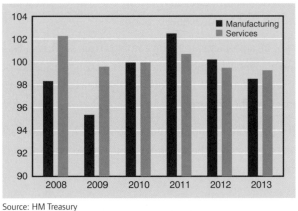

Source: HM Treasury

● A strong manufacturing sector can also stimulate a culture of innovation and investment. This is linked to the point above: the possibility of high returns from capital spending acts as an incentive for firms to spend on research and development (R&D) which can be a key driver of long-run, supply-side growth for the macroeconomy.

● Finally, manufacturing still accounts for 60% of the value of UK exports. The pattern of exports of goods from the UK (see Figure 3.5) gives a clear indication of the competitiveness and value of the manufacturing sectors of the UK economy.

Figure 3.5: UK exports of manufactured goods in 2013, £bn (sectors with value >£0.2bn only)

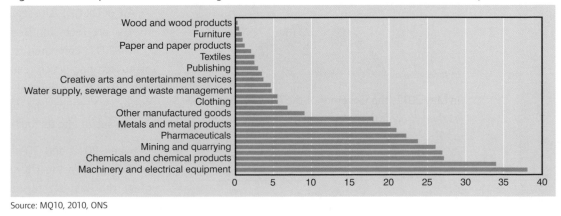

Source: MQ10, 2010, ONS

- The UK clearly still enjoys a strong position as an exporter of manufactured goods such as chemicals and fibres and transport and electrical equipment. In addition, manufacturing activity creates jobs in related service sector industries such as transport, distribution and finance. The UK does still enjoy world dominance in some sectors, such as the production of Formula 1 cars and other high-technology industries.

Between August 2013 and August 2014 there was a 3.9% increase in manufacturing output in the UK, with increases in 10 of the 13 manufacturing sectors and strongest growth in rubber and plastic products and other non-metallic mineral products.

However, there are other arguments regarding the importance, and even desirability, of sustaining UK manufacturing to consider.

Figure 3.6: UK net profitability (net rate of return) secondary and tertiary sector

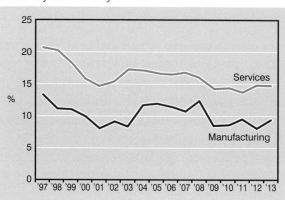

Source: ONS

- Figure 3.6 compares the net profitability of manufacturing and service sector forms in the UK since 1997. Profitability – the ability of firms to turn capital employed into profit – is higher in the service sector, and the differential has widened in recent years.

- Export-led growth may not improve the current account position significantly if UK production depends on imported raw materials or even, in some cases, off-shored and outsourced production and services.

- Policies to boost UK production of manufactures may distort the market and lead to resources being wasted on relatively expensive and relatively low quality goods.

- A trade deficit in goods need not be a problem providing earnings from services, investment income and transfers are sufficient to create an overall balance on the current account. Thus support which might be given to the manufacturing sector might be more efficiently utilised in bolstering already strong competitive advantages in service sector industries.

- Arguably, structural shifts in the UK economy moving production away from manufacturing and towards services represent strong market forces which the UK and its policy-makers are powerless to totally resist (see the next section on the service sector).

● ● **Knowledge and Application: The growth of the service sector**

Figure 3.7: Service sector industries

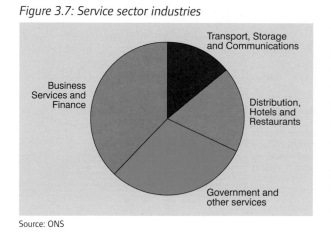

Source: ONS

Service sector output in 2011 accounted for 78.4% of UK GDP. The service sector returned to its pre-recession level of output in Q3 of 2011, compared to construction and manufacturing which remained almost 10% below the Q1 2008 peak as of June 2014. Figure 3.7 shows the breakdown of the service sector into its four sectors.

Between 2013 and 2014, the two largest contributors to the UK service sector also grew the fastest: business services and finance (4.8%) and distribution, hotels and restaurants (3.7%). Overall, service sector output rose 3.4% between 2013 and 2014.

Question

1. What factors could explain why service sector productivity is typically higher than manufacturing productivity?

● ● Knowledge and Application: Investment in the UK

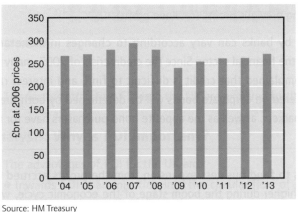

Figure 3.8: UK investment (Gross Fixed Capital Formation)

Source: HM Treasury

Investment plays a crucial role in any economy. As a significant component of aggregate demand, investment spending contributes to GDP and therefore the overall health of the macroeconomy through creating output and jobs. Investment is also a key driver of long-run trend growth, increasing productivity and productive potential. The key measure of investment is Fixed Capital Investment: spending on producer goods (or capital goods) such as machinery, ICT and plant which is then used to produce consumer goods or other producer goods.

● Analysis: Why is investment volatile?

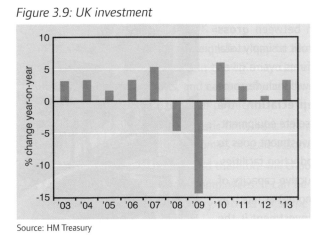

Figure 3.9: UK investment

Source: HM Treasury

Investment levels in the economy are seen by economists as an important indicator of the future expectations of firms. If business confidence is strong, firms are prepared to commit spending to increasing their production and supply potential. But when confidence is weak they will stop new investment projects (and even in extreme cases, mothball current projects) as they anticipate flat or falling demand in the future. Figure 3.9 shows the annual percentage change in investment levels over the same period as that shown in Figure 3.8. Invest-

ment levels fall by almost 5% in 2008, followed by a drop of over 10% in 2009. Investment in 2009 had fallen by 18% in real terms from its peak in 2007, reducing the contribution made to GDP by investment from 17.3% to 15%.

Investment spending tends to be more volatile than other components of GDP, such as consumption and government spending, for various reasons:

● The accelerator effect

Investment spending often reacts more quickly and more dramatically than spending by households and the public sector. This was discussed in more detail in Chapter 2, where causes of the fall in consumer spending in 2008-09 is discussed. In brief, firms can reduce investment more easily than households can do with consumer spending. A high proportion of household consumption, particularly for those on lower

● Membership of the European Union, meaning any output exported from the UK to other EU countries is classed as a British export and therefore is not subject to the Common External Tariff (import tax).

● The UK labour market is more flexible and lightly regulated than in many other European economies, making it easier and cheaper for MNCs to recruit workers here.

Other factors which can increase inward FDI are agglomeration effects ('clusters' of economic activity which attract related and complementary firms, such as hi-tech industries and tourism) and imperfect competition (the potential for monopoly power implies higher future profits, provided barriers to entry to the sector can be maintained).

The recession in 2008 then led to considerably reduced inward FDI in 2009 before recovering later, possibly because these challenging macroeconomic conditions were experienced throughout the EU and the UK remained an attractive place to invest. Relative to the performance of 'the PIIGS' (Portugal, Ireland, Italy, Greece and Spain), the UK has arguably gained a competitive advantage.

Some economists have argued that although Britain's position inside the EU is a strength in attracting FDI, its reluctance to adopt the single European currency (the euro) is a weakness. In the light of the uncertain future of the eurozone (see Chapter 12) this argument needs less consideration.

Other weaknesses perceived for the UK are:

● A rising tax burden, which makes the UK a less attractive place to work and do business.

● An increase in business bureaucracy ('red-tape').

Figure 3.11: Where does UK inward FDI come from? (2010)

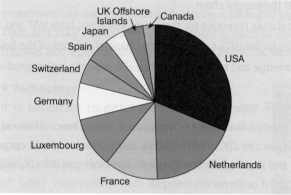

Source: ONS

Figure 3.12: Where does UK outward FDI take place? (2010)

Source: ONS

Again, this needs to be viewed in the context of other Western European economies which tend to have similar, if not more restrictive, business environments.

In recent years there has been growing interest in the growth of sovereign wealth funds. This is usually oil revenue which creates wealth for economies such as Saudi Arabia or Norway, which can then be used to invest in global business opportunities. Interestingly, Figure 3.11 shows that the major contributors to UK inward FDI are none of the rapidly growing BRIC countries or major oil-producing nations.

Figure 3.12 shows the pattern of UK outwards FDI.

For both inward and outward flows, the EU, North America and Japan account for almost all of the top ten countries shown.

Question

3. Does it matter that the BRIC nations and the oil-producing countries are not major sources of inward FDI to the UK?

● ● Knowledge and Application: The UK stock market

The performance of the UK stock market in recent years was shown in Figure 1.11 in Chapter 1. The stock market offers an insight into the performance of the largest firms in the economy, most of which have

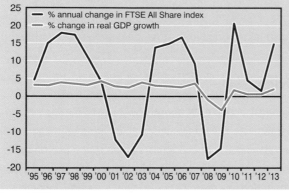

Figure 3.13: Real GDP growth and stock market performance for the UK

Source: HM Treasury

publicly-owned shares. These shares (which are a *share* of ownership, and entitle holders to a *share* of the profits made) are traded on the stock market. Aggregate measures such as the FTSE indices show how the values of those firms are changing, based mainly on their fundamental ability to generate future profits. Therefore we might expect stock market performance to correlate closely with overall macroeconomic performance, measured best as real GDP growth. Figure 3.13 shows the movement in real GDP growth in the UK with the annual change in stock market prices.

Stock market volatility tends to be far greater than growth volatility. This trend has persisted throughout history, and was named 'animal spirits' by John Maynard Keynes: a form of herd behaviour where speculators over-react to the potential gains, and losses, in rapidly changing asset markets. This can be contrasted with the 'wisdom of crowds' theory, where aggregate opinions and behaviours are seen as more perceptive and rational than individual decisions.

The '**bull markets**' of 1996-2000 and 2004-07 can be viewed with hindsight as examples of stock market bubbles, and fit into the wider picture presented in Chapter 1 of a period of very high consumption growth in the UK, fuelled by wealth effects from the housing market and stock markets. When UK (and global) growth appeared to falter after the 2000 dot-com crash, the UK stock market fell dramatically (this is known as a '**bear market**'), before recovering strongly in the years before the credit crisis and recession at the end of the 2000s.

Interestingly, the percentage loss experienced on the FTSE index in 2002 was just as severe as that seen in 2008, when the UK economy was in recession. At the end of 2003 the FTSE All Share Index stood at less than 2000, compared with 2329 in December 2009 and 3427 in December 2013.

Stock markets had increased steadily through 2013 and 2014 in both the UK and USA but the markets saw significant drops in October 2014 against increasing threats of a Eurozone recession and slowing growth in emerging economies.

Question

4. Figure 3.13 shows the volatile character of stock market prices compared with the growth in the real economy. To explain this greater volatility the stockmarket has been described as "a market not in the present but in the future". How does that description help to account for the contrasting data in Figure 3.13?

Chapter 4
Living Standards, Poverty and Inequality

This chapter examines the changes in living standards over the past decade, looking at various measures of living standards. Measures of inequality and poverty are then examined, along with trends in inequality and poverty over the past decade. Following this there is a discussion on recent government policy to tackle poverty and inequality, concluding with a look at regional differences within the UK.

● Knowledge: **Standard of living**

There is considerable debate amongst economists about how best to measure standard of living. Many factors influence people's living standards. These include social, environmental, and political factors as well as economic ones. However, the vast majority of economists agree that a person or household's income is a very important determinant of living standards. National **income** is the sum of all the earnings received through employing factors of production in a given period of time. Crucially, income is a **flow** of payments. Income to a household could be in the form of wages, salaries, profits, interest payments, rents or other forms of payments received such as state benefits and pensions.

● Application: **The rise and then 'squeeze' on living standards in the last decade**

Figure 4.1: Growth in UK real household disposable income

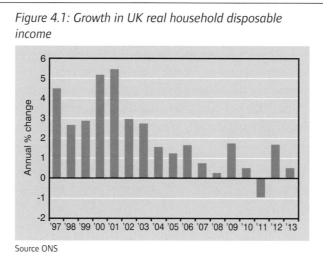

Source ONS

'Real' household income growth is the growth in household income received accounting for the effects of inflation year on year. So the data in Figure 4.1 shows the rate at which the average household's purchasing power has changed over the last 17 years. During the late 1990s, during the Labour government's first term in office, real household incomes grew rapidly, but there was a marked slowdown in real income growth from 2002 onwards. Perhaps the most surprising part of the data above is that average real household incomes continued to grow during the 'Great Recession' of 2008-09, when GDP and employment fell considerably. During these two years, household incomes were supported by a combination of growth in income from tax credits and state benefits, along with stable employment income and low inflation (according to the RPI index inflation was actually negative in 2009). However, the effects of the recession were delayed, not evaded. As the recovery faltered in 2010 and unemployment rose above 8%, workers had little bargaining power and average wage growth has remained anaemic ever since. Many workers accepted pay cuts or pay freezes. In addition, high cost-push inflationary pressures from rising petrol, food, clothing and energy prices eroded real household incomes. In September 2011 CPI inflation reached 5.2%, but then it fell sharply towards the 2.0% target by mid-2012. From early 2013 the recovery finally took hold, raising hopes that real income growth might be restored.

However, despite strong jobs growth and falling unemployment in 2013-14, nominal wage growth remained stubbornly low, going against the historical norm for recoveries and puzzling many economists. In fact, average weekly earnings were 0.2 per cent lower in the three months to June 2014 than in the same period a year earlier, the first time that has happened since the depths of the recession in 2009. Sustained increases in real wages have remained elusive, and with it the squeeze on living standards continues despite strong employment growth in 2013-14. Explanations of this phenomenon include low productivity growth in the UK, and firms and workers preferring to keep employment levels high instead of raising pay, as they are unwilling to shed talent and lose their investment in training, though there is no consensus.

Although there are various ways in which living standards can be measured, real GDP per capita is the measure most commonly used by economists. There are however, limitations to the use of this measure. These include:

- No account taken for the distribution of income and wealth – GDP per capita is a crude 'mean' measure, and so it might not give an accurate reflection of the income of an 'average' person in a country, especially if income is distributed unevenly. If a large share of national income is concentrated at the top end of the income distribution, then the mean GDP per capita figure will be higher than the true income of the 'average' person. Therefore, a measure of median income might be a better reflection of the income of an 'average' person.

- No account taken for externalities – growth often occurs with resulting negative externalities (e.g. pollution) but these are not accounted for in GDP figures. In fact, the expense of cleaning up pollution may even add *positively* to GDP figures. Thus, growth in GDP may overstate the resultant rise in living standards.

- Quality changes ignored – over time the quality of goods and services tend to increase but these are not accounted for in GDP figures. Therefore, rises in the quality of goods and services (e.g. safer cars, better quality TVs etc.) means that increases in living standards may be greater than a crude GDP per capita measure suggests.

- No account taken for the 'balance' of growth – growth based on consumption today may take available resources away from investment, which would bring faster growth tomorrow. The UK economy has become very dependant on consumption, as mentioned in Chapter 1. Since the financial crisis policy makers have emphasised the importance of a 'rebalancing' of the economy away from consumption and importing, towards investment and exports.

- Exports are valued more highly than imports – In GDP statistics the value of exports is added to GDP while the value of imports is subtracted from GDP, as shown in the formula C + I + G + (X-M). So, according to GDP data imports subtract from living standards, which plainly isn't true in many cases. If UK citizens enjoy a foreign made car, or some fine French wine, in reality this will add to, rather than detract from, living standards.

- No account taken for non-marketed items – if you carry out some DIY work on your home, or someone babysits for you free of charge, these services will not be counted in GDP statistics, but if you pay for these (or similar services), they will be counted.

- No account taken for the opportunity cost of growth – in order to create growth leisure time may be foregone. By working longer hours GDP may increase, but living standards might not.

- Admin errors are likely – GDP data is calculated using tax returns from millions of sources. There are bound to be errors and inaccuracies in the data.

Exam Hint

When answering an exam question it may be relevant to explain how some of the limitations of using GDP data to estimate living standards. It is better to go for **depth** over **breadth**. Pick two or three limitations and explain them in detail, rather than explaining five limitations superficially.

Alternative measures to income

The material 'standard of living' can be contrasted with '**quality of life**' which accounts for other, more intangible factors that affect human life, such health, environmental quality, safety, social life, culture etc. Attempts to measure quality of life intend to give a better indicator of people's overall '**well-being**'.

The **Genuine Progress indicator** (**GPI**) is an extension of the **Index of Sustainable Economic Welfare** (**ISEW**). The GPI aims to account for the costs of the negative consequences of economic growth, as well as the positive impacts, and hence give a more balanced account of how the overall well being of a country's citizens have changed over time. The measure accounts for factors that the GDP measure ignores, such as:

- Cost of resource depletion

- Cost of crime

- Cost of ozone depletion

- Cost of family breakdown

- Cost of air, water, and noise pollution

- Loss of farmland

- Loss of wetlands

With such emphasis placed on environmental as well as social factors, it is unsurprising that the GPI is a popular measure amongst 'green' economists. The ISEW and GPI indicators show a diverging trend from the GDP measure since the 1970s for most rich economies, including the UK. The GPI failed to increase significantly since the 1970s, suggesting that rising incomes since the 1970s has come at the expense of high and unsustainable environmental and social costs, meaning that growth is now failing to add to the well-being of citizens in advanced economies. Of course, accurately measuring the cost of family breakdown and global warming is extremely difficult, and this is something that neo-classical economists point to when defending the GDP measure.

The United Nations first published the **Human Development Index** (**HDI**) in 1990. The HDI is composed of three indicators, and countries are given a score between 0 and 1. The indicators include:

- Real GDP per capita (using Purchasing Power Parity).

- Life expectancy at birth (to indicate the population's level of health and longevity).

- Educational attainment (measured using a weighted average of adult literacy rates and the gross enrolment ratio at primary, secondary and tertiary education level).

Table 4.1: Selected HDI and GDP per capita data

Country	HDI value (2013)	HDI ranking	GDP per capita (PPP$) 2012	GDP per capita ranking	GDP per capita – HDI ranking
Norway	0.944	1	62,858	6	5
Australia	0.933	2	42,278	15	13
United States	0.914	5	50,859	9	4
UK	0.892	14	34,694	27	13
South Africa	0.658	118	11,989	79	-39
Cuba	0.815	44	*18,796	55	11
China	0.719	91	10,771	88	-3

Source: UN Human Development Report 2014   *2011

In Table 4.1 the final column showing the GDP per capita rank minus the HDI ranking for different countries is one way of examining whether higher incomes result in a higher quality of life for the citizens of that country. It is clearly not always the case that this occurs. South Africa has a GDP per capita ranking 39 places higher than its HDI ranking. This is due to the high rates of HIV/AIDS coupled with very high unemployment and poverty rates which reduce life expectancy considerably. Cuba has a low ranking for GDP per capita owing to an inefficient command economy. However, Cuba's HDI ranking is 11 places higher due to an extensive literacy campaign and substantial public investment in healthcare. The UK's performance in the HDI rankings is hindered by a lower average number of years of schooling than other advanced economies.

Evaluation of HDI as an indicator of living standards

Advantages	Disadvantages
The HDI goes beyond crude GDP measurements with all the associated limitations to incorporate statistics on education and healthcare, two key development goals.	The HDI is an aggregate measure which hides distribution.
The publishing of this indicator encourages countries to invest in education and healthcare.	Aggregate measures do little to tell us why HDI may have changed over time.
Unlike GDP an element of 'well being' is reflected in the statistics.	Wouldn't quality-adjusted life years (QALYs) be a better measure than simply the average number of years lived?
The HDI does not include too many indices and thus the problem of overlap is avoided e.g. infant mortality is not included but its importance is reflected in the life expectancy indicator.	Shouldn't the quality of education be included, rather than just years in schooling? The UK has some of the best universities in the world, but this is not accounted for in the HDI measure.
The indices used are relatively easy to measure e.g. no value has to be placed on the cost of global warming.	Weightings given (equal for all 3 indicators) are fairly arbitrary. Some argue that income should be given more importance.
The UN now calculates the HDI to distinguish between regions, genders, and ethnic groups, thus avoiding 'broad brush' conclusions to be drawn based on aggregates.	The HDI may overstate development in countries with high inequality (e.g. Latin American countries) as aggregates mask the low quality of life endured by a large number.

In *A Better Quality of Life*, published in 1999 the Government committed itself to reporting annually on progress made towards sustainable development in the UK.

> "Talking about sustainable development is not enough. We have to know what it is, to see how our policies are working on the ground. We must hold ourselves to account – as a government but also as a country... All this depends on devising new ways of assessing how we are doing."
>
> **Tony Blair**, *Prime Minister*
> *A Better Quality of Life – A Strategy for Sustainable Development for the UK*, May 1999

The government introduced 13 new headline indicators of quality of life: economic growth, social investment, employment, health, education and training, housing quality, climate change, air pollution, transport, water quality, wildlife, land use and finally waste.

Figure 4.5: Real UK income growth by percentile point, 2007-08 to 2012-13

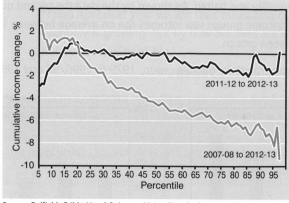

Source: Belfield, Cribb, Hood & Joyce, *Living Standards, Inequality and Poverty in the UK 2014*, IFS

fell. However, the 2011-12 to 2012-13 line shows that inequality changed very little during the most recent year from the data, and if real earnings growth does take hold as the economy recovers, and planned welfare reforms such as benefit cuts are carried out, the trend of falling inequality seen over the 5 years from 2007-08 to 2012-13 could be halted or reversed.

Question

2. How might economists compare income inequality **between** countries?

● ● Application **and** Analysis: **The Gini coefficient system**

Figure 4.6: The Gini coefficient, 1977 to 2012/13

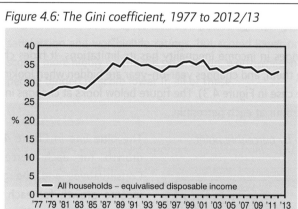

Source: ONS

Figure 4.7: 50/10, 90/50, and 99/90 ratios

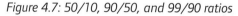
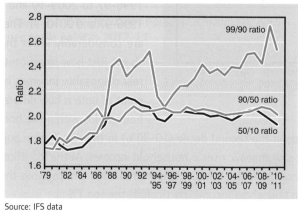

Source: IFS data

The Gini coefficient is a commonly used statistical measure of income inequality. The Gini coefficient gives a number between 0 and 1, where 0 represents prefect equality, and 1 represents perfect inequality (all the income goes to one household). The measure takes into account all of the income distribution.

Another common measure of inequality is the ratio of the income of one particular percentile to another. It is simply the ratio of the household income at a certain percentile expressed as a ratio of the household income of a selected lower percentile. This measure is particularly useful because it compares just two points in the distribution. As can be seen from Figure 4.7, although there was a broad-based rise in inequality between percentiles in the 1980s, income inequality between most households has remained fairly constant since the early 1990s, with lower income households actually moving closer to median household income. However, the very top earners have pulled away significantly, even from relatively well-off households, as shown by the rise in the 99/90 ratio since the mid-1990s.

● ● Application **and** Analysis: **Recent trends in income inequality and their causes**

Trying to get a comprehensive picture about trends in income inequality is difficult and this is why it is important to look at a number of measures as data on **overall** income inequality can mask changes **within** the income distribution. Given the data above, there are a number of conclusions that we can draw about income inequality in the UK. The causes of these changes are also explained.

1979-1990: Rising inequality

It is clear from all measures that there was a rapid and widespread increase in income inequality during the 1980s. The Gini coefficient rose from 0.26 to 0.34 during the decade, and Figure 4.3 shows that under the Conservative governments of 1979-97 the higher the level of income, the higher the rate of income growth.

There are several underlying reasons for the rapid rise in inequality during this period:

1. *Technology and demand for skills* – Earnings (or 'original income') inequality grew rapidly. Technological change reduced demand for low skilled workers in a number of industries (e.g. computers can do much of the work of clerks). At the same time, advanced technology has made skilled workers who can effectively use the new technology more productive, thus raising their reward through higher wages (e.g. accountants can use computer programmes to raise their output).

2. *Rapid deindustrialisation* through removing state support for heavy industry reduced the demand for lots of workers in these industries. Structural unemployment affected many, and male participation in the workforce declined, reducing the incomes of these households.

3. The 1980s saw a rapid rise in *female participation* in the workforce. This led to a widening gap between no-earner and two-earner households.

4. Spurred on by government initiatives to encourage entrepreneurship, the number of *self-employed workers grew rapidly*. As the variation in the earnings of self-employed workers is higher than for all workers, earnings inequality grew overall.

5. In 1981 *state benefits became linked to inflation* rather than earnings. As earnings tend to rise more quickly than prices those on benefits saw their incomes fall behind the incomes of those in work.

6. Government policies to *reduce the power of trade unions* meant less wage bargaining power for (usually) relatively low paid workers in many industries.

7. Dramatic *cuts in top rates of income tax* increased the disposable incomes of those at the top, while the switch to a *greater level of indirect taxation* significantly reduced the real incomes of those with lower incomes, thus widening inequality.

1990-97: Stable, slightly falling inequality

From 1990 to 1997 inequality remained historically high but fell very slightly overall, as shown by the Gini coefficient in Figure 4.6. There are a number of reasons for this:

1. The rapid economic growth of the mid to late 1980s which caused the earnings of those at the top to pull away from the rest was not prevalent during this period. The early 90s recession and aftermath caused the incomes of higher earners to suffer, as shown by the significant fall in the 99/90 ratio from 1992 to 1995/6 in Figure 4.7.

2. Direct taxation was increased in the early 1990s, hitting the richest the hardest.

3. Means-tested benefits were introduced in the early 1990s, giving more help to low earners who were in true need of financial help.

1997-2004/5: Generally stable overall inequality, convergence for most, divergence at the top and bottom

Under Labour, from 1997 to 2004-05 the overall level of inequality remained roughly stable, fluctuating between 0.34 and 0.35. However, the most notable changes during this period were changes within the income distribution. The 99/90 ratio in Figure 4.7 shows that the incomes of the top earners grew much quicker in this period than the income of other households during this period. However, the 90/50 ratio shows that the income gap between the 90th and 50th percentiles remained fairly constant. At the same time, Figure 4.4 shows that under Labour the bottom percentile were the only group who saw their real

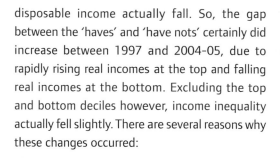

disposable income actually fall. So, the gap between the 'haves' and 'have nots' certainly did increase between 1997 and 2004-05, due to rapidly rising real incomes at the top and falling real incomes at the bottom. Excluding the top and bottom deciles however, income inequality actually fell slightly. There are several reasons why these changes occurred:

1. The *process of globalisation* was rapid and powerful during this period. As UK companies expanded their operations to overseas markets, the actions of top managers could,

Inequality has fallen recently but that may only be temporary.

arguably, raise the value they added to their companies, and thus higher salaries could be justified. Furthermore, in a more globalised economy demand for highly skilled labour including top managers, architects, engineers etc. is very high (just think about the demand for these workers in places like Dubai and Kuwait), and thus the salaries of highly-skilled labour grew.

2. The New Labour government cracked down on workers claiming benefits, and incapacity benefit in particular, by *tightening the eligibility criteria for benefits*. In addition the government clamped down on those claiming benefits that they deemed to be capable of work. This caused the income of some at the bottom of the distribution to fall.

3. *Public sector employment* grew dramatically under New Labour (by around 850,000). *Pay awards* for public sector workers *exceeded inflation* during this period, and thus the real incomes of a growing number of public sector workers increased considerably, helping many in low paid public sector jobs to catch up with median household income.

4. One of the first pieces of legislation passed by the Labour government was the introduction of the *minimum wage*. The minimum wage increased faster than the rate of inflation during this period, thus boosting the real incomes of those in work on low pay, helping to close the gap to median earnings.

5. The introduction of *tax credits* for working families on low income helped to increase the real disposable incomes of many households.

6. During this period *unemployment fell* considerably, from 2.18 million at the beginning of 1997 to 1.43 million at the beginning of 2005. This fall meant that many at the lower end of the income distribution saw their incomes grow as they gained employment.

7. *National Insurance Contributions* (*NICs*), which are broadly progressive, increased from 2003 which reduced the inequality of disposable household incomes.

2004/5-2008/9: Rising income inequality

From 2004-05 to 2008-09 there was a general rise in income inequality, with the Gini coefficient, 99/90 and 90/50 ratios all increasing. This suggests a significant increase in inequality spread across the distribution, although high earners saw particularly strong income growth during this period. This rise in inequality occurred due to:

1. From mid-2005 *unemployment started to rise*, causing a fall in the incomes of those who lost their jobs.

2. From 2004-05 until the beginning of 2008 *share prices and company profits* were rising considerably. Therefore bankers, traders and company bosses increased their pay packets (including bonuses) in line with this, raising incomes at the top end.

3. In 2004 the *EU expanded* to include 10 new member states from Central and Eastern Europe. The UK was one of just 3 of the existing EU members who allowed open access to their labour market for migrant

workers from the accession states. The UK government estimated that around 40,000 migrants would come to the UK from the new EU members, but by the end of the decade around 1 million had arrived. The productive migrant workers were willing to work for relatively little pay, putting downward pressure on wages in mostly unskilled, low paid jobs. Although this helped to control wage inflation in the economy, it hindered the wage growth of relatively unskilled workers in the UK.

2008/9-2014: A dramatic fall in income inequality or a one off?

From 2008-09 to 2012-13 a mixed picture emerges. Figure 4.7 shows that the 90/50 and 50/10 ratios all fell from 2008-09. In addition, Figure 4.5 shows that during the troubled years of 2007-08 to 2012-13 higher income groups saw significantly larger falls in real income than any other group, over a fall of 8% for the highest percentiles, while the lowest percentile groups saw small increases in their real income. All this suggests a fall in income inequality.

However, the 99/90 ratio increased dramatically between 2008-09 and 2009-10, suggesting rapid income growth for high earners (which is explained below). This explains why the Gini coefficient didn't fall despite the fall in the 90/50 ratio. However, from 2010-11 inequality fell according to all measures, and quite significantly. The Gini coefficient fell from 0.36 to 0.34 in a single year. The fall in income for high earners was a major contributing factor to this fall in inequality. There are several reasons for these changes:

1. The rapid rise in the income of those at the top of the distribution between 2008-09 to 2009-10 was due to high earners bringing income forward (known as *'forestalling'*) in order *to avoid the new 50% income tax rate on income* above £150,000 which was introduced by the Labour government and came into effect in April 2010. This meant that although incomes at the top end grew dramatically from 2008-09 to 2009-10, they then fell considerably from 2009-10, causing the Gini coefficient to fall by some way.

2. Real disposable incomes at the bottom rose significantly from 2008-09 to 2010-11 due to rises in tax credits and state benefits higher than the rate of inflation, which fell dramatically due to the recession. As earnings growth from 2009 onwards was extremely low, and negative in real terms for many, out of work benefits increased at a faster rate than earnings, causing a fall in real income inequality.

3. Despite the effects of forestalling in 2009-10, the incomes of those at the top have been hit the hardest by the Great Recession and its aftermath. As shown in Figure 4.5: the higher the level of income, the greater the fall in real incomes from 2007 to 2013. Some estimates suggest that the real incomes of the top 1% have fallen by 15% since the full effects of the financial crisis were felt. The UK economy has a very large financial services sector (roughly 10% of GDP), and workers in this sector tend to have high pay. In the aftermath of the financial crisis employment in the City of London fell by 7%, which has put downward pressure on pay in the sector. In addition poor macroeconomic conditions from 2008 to 2013 have meant that there is less justification for large bonuses in the financial sector and in the board room as share prices and company profits have struggled. Also, negative media attention and public opinion over 'excessive' executive pay has constrained the pay of top earners. Shareholder revolts have also put the brakes on boardroom pay.

Perhaps the most notable point to make is not the changes in UK income inequality that have occurred in the last decade, but the **level** of income inequality which is very high by historical standards, and high compared to most other advanced European economies. Many of the underlying causes of rising inequality in the 1980s are still prevalent as reasons for higher levels of inequality in the UK today, and earnings or 'original' income inequality remains high as the labour market rewards highly skilled workers much more than those with few skills. The Gini coefficient rose in the year to 2012-13 as shown in Figure 4.6, and Figure 4.7 shows that from 2011-12 to 2012-13, real income growth of the highest earners was back to being broadly in line with other groups, while the real incomes of those on the lowest income fell considerably. This supports the view that despite the fall in income inequality following the Great Recession this trend is unlikely to last in the long term, as the underlying causes of high inequality remain.

● Knowledge: **The case for and against inequality**

Free market economists argue that inequality is necessary for the efficient functioning of the economy. Workers are paid according to their productivity, and therefore this creates the incentive for workers to work hard. Without the rewards of higher earnings workers would be less productive, and the threat of economic hardship for those who don't work hard makes the economy more productive, encouraging growth and efficiency. Furthermore, free market economists say that inequality is justified as different workers add different levels of value to their employer. If a good CEO performs well and makes decisions which add an extra £300 million to their company's revenue, then it is justified for them to be paid more than a secretary at the same company as their value added is considerably less.

Critics of this free market approach argue that inequality is not justified as all workers are part of the wealth creation process, not just the entrepreneurial class. Furthermore, in their book *The Spirit Level* which attracted a great deal of attention Wilkinson and Pickett provide evidence to suggest that societies with greater levels of inequality suffer from resultant negative externalities such as higher levels of crime, worse public health, and lower social cohesion. In 2014 the Equality Trust thinktank estimated that the cost of inequality, through its impact on health, wellbeing and crime rates, to be £39bn per year. In addition to the external costs of inequality, there is the argument that people on lower incomes spend a higher proportion of their income. Redistribution from higher to lower income groups will therefore increase overall consumption and output.

Question

3. Income inequality has been in the spotlight since the 2008 financial crisis and the subsequent recession. To what extent is the UK's current level of inequality damaging for growth and overall social welfare?

There is clear evidence that the overall level of inequality in the UK has not fallen since 1997 despite efforts by the Labour and Coalition governments to redistribute income. The tax and benefit system is redistributive by nature. The incomes of the richest after taxes and benefits are lower than before, and the incomes of the poorest after taxes and benefits are higher.

Table 4.2: The effects of taxes and benefits on household income

Original income (wages, salaries, self-employment income, pensions, investment income)		
add Cash Benefits	= **Gross income**	
subtract Direct taxes and NICs	= **Disposable income**	
subtract Indirect taxes	= **Post tax income**	
add Benefits in kind (e.g. NHS)	= **Final income**	

In 2010/11 the top quintile of households had an average original income 16 times greater than the bottom quintile (£81,500 compared to £5,100). After taxes and benefits the average income of the top quintile was just four times greater than that of the bottom quintile (£61,400 compared to £15,200).

Direct taxes are taxes which are levied directly on an individual or organisation e.g. income tax. Most direct taxes are **progressive**, meaning that the higher the level of income the greater the proportion of income is taken in tax. Indirect taxes are taxes paid on expenditure on goods and services e.g. VAT, tobacco duty. Indirect taxes are **regressive**, meaning that the higher the level of income the lower the proportion of income is taken in tax. The tax system in the UK overall does little to redistribute income. The benefit system is far more redistributive. Although some cash benefits are **universal** such as the state pension, many are **means-tested** such as income support, and as of 2013, child benefit, which had previously been universal. The change was made as part of the government's deficit reduction strategy.

● ● Analysis and Evaluation: Government policies to tackle inequality and work poverty

Several policies have been introduced to address inequality and we summarise the key measures.

- The **National Minimum Wage (NMW)** – came into effect in 1999 and since then the government have increased the NMW faster than the rates of both inflation and earnings in most years. For 2014 the rate for workers aged 21 and over stood at £6.50, while it was at £5.13 for 18-20 year olds and £3.79 for those under 18. Supporters of the NMW claim that it reduces poverty and worker exploitation. At the same time it provides a strong incentive for people to work, thus reducing the unemployment and poverty traps.

The NMW has its critics from the right and left of the political spectrum. Some critics of the NMW say that despite large and growing differences in living costs between regions, there is no regional variation in the NMW. In London where the cost of living is highest there has been a campaign for employers to adopt a London 'Living Wage' which stood at £8.80 per hour in 2014. The Living Wage Foundation says this is the lowest wage that allows people to meet the cost of living, and was set at £7.65 for the rest of the UK in 2014. The Living Wage has been supported by all of the main political parties but it is voluntary, and not legally binding. Critics also point out that although the NMW did not appear to cause unemployment during the NICE decade, during the subsequent recession, when businesses were less willing to hire workers the NMW could have had a negative impact on employment.

- **The Working and Children's Tax Credits** – Both came into effect in April 2003 to divide the old Working Families Tax Credit into two parts.

The Child Tax Credit can be claimed by people who are responsible for children regardless of whether they are in or out of work. Households on lower income receive a greater amount through the Child Tax Credit system.

The main aim of the Working Tax Credit is to 'make work pay'. Those on low incomes with or without children are able to claim this tax credit. The scheme is designed to improve the incentive to work, thus increasing participation rates and reducing the poverty trap. The poverty trap is where a worker, often working part time, has no incentive to work harder or for longer, as this would result in benefits being lost (e.g. free school meals for children) and a greater amount being taken in tax. Thus, the very high effective marginal tax rate discourages work. The Working Tax Credit also reduces the unemployment trap by increasing the rewards from work over the income from benefits.

However, the tax credit system is not without its criticisms:

- There will always be a 'withdrawal zone', where benefits are being removed as incomes rise. The existence of this zone provides less of an incentive to work more hours, or take better jobs.
- Tax credits cost the Treasury around £25bn per annum, an enormous cost.
- The system is very complex, and thus there is a large administrative cost associated with the level of bureaucracy. Furthermore, many applying for tax credits complain about the difficulty of the forms that need to be filled in. This complexity has caused the 'take-up rate' for the Working Tax Credit in particular, to be low, at just 61% in 2009/10 according to the HMRC. Furthermore, the complex nature of the system has led to administrative mistakes, with the HMRC overpaying claimants by some £6bn between 2003 and 2007. Fraud has also been a serious problem.

- **The introduction of the 50% top rate of income tax** – In April 2010 a new 50% top rate of income tax was introduced on incomes above £150,000. The Chancellor Alistair Darling introduced the top rate as an 'emergency measure' in his April 2009 budget. It was intended to raise £6bn in tax revenue, as well as reducing income inequality. However, the HMRC estimate that it has raised very little, and Chancellor George Osborne announced in his March 2012 budget that the top rate of income tax would be cut to 45% in April 2013, where it has remained.

- **The New Deal (known as the 'Flexible New Deal' from 2009)** – This programme is aimed at providing training, subsidised employment and voluntary work for the unemployed, thus providing them with the skills necessary to obtain a job. Furthermore, the New Deal introduced the ability to withdraw benefits from those who refused 'reasonable employment'.

- **Government funding of apprenticeships** – there has been widespread cross-party support for greater funding of apprenticeships which are seen as a good way of providing people with the skills employers demand and reducing skills shortages in various sectors. However, four out of five companies claim they face barriers to hiring apprentices such as administrative issues and employer's liability insurance.

- **Improving 'in kind' benefits** – the funding of education and healthcare has increased considerably since 1997. Better education and healthcare should help the poorest proportionally more, as it means they should have the level of health and skills that are necessary to be rewarded in the labour market, thus reducing inter-generational poverty.

- **Cutting the basic rate of income tax** – in 2007 the Chancellor Gordon Brown cut the basic rate of income tax from 22% to 20%, claiming that this would increase the disposable incomes of many low income families. However, to fund this, he scrapped the lower 10% rate, meaning that many of the poorest families actually saw a fall in their overall disposable incomes. This drew sharp criticism and the government extended tax credits to try to offset the effects of the tax change.

- **Increasing the tax free personal allowance** – one of the main redistributive policies of the Coalition government has been to raise the personal allowance (how much taxable income you can have before you start paying Income Tax) from £6,475 in 2009-10 to £10,000 in 2014-15. This was a key feature of the Liberal Democrat election manifesto in 2010. This has partly been funded by meagre increases in the higher 40% tax threshold, with rises in the threshold falling well behind inflation, causing what's known as 'fiscal drag'. Following the 2014-15 budget it has been estimated that 1.1m more people pay some of their income at the higher 40% tax rate than would have under Labour's published plans in 2010. As a result of these changes, lower income households are better off overall, while higher income households pay a higher proportion of their income in tax.

- **The Winter Fuel Payment and fuel poverty** – The allowance, first introduced in the winter of 1997/98 was aimed at reducing the level fuel poverty amongst the elderly. Since then however, the payment has been made universal in the sense that it can be claimed by any household with a member over the age of 60. Critics say the measure is very costly for the Treasury, and poorly targeted.

Despite these measures, there is widespread concern that the Coalition government's policy of favouring spending cuts over tax increases to reduce the budget deficit will affect poorer, more vulnerable households the most, as public services and benefit payments are continually squeezed. With austerity measures projected to continue until at least 2018, low income households may continue to see their relative position decline in the years ahead.

●● Knowledge and Application: The distribution of wealth in the UK

Unlike income which is a flow, wealth is a **stock** concept. Household wealth is the total value of assets owned by the household at a point in time. Marketable wealth incorporates physical wealth such as houses, land and cars, as well as financial wealth such as financial assets like shares and bonds. Non-marketable wealth (wealth that cannot be sold to anyone else) mainly consists of pension rights. Wealth is usually more unevenly distributed than income, as it is accumulated over a lifetime. Those on higher incomes are able to accumulate wealth through savings, buying shares, getting a mortgage to purchase a house etc. whereas those on lower incomes will struggle to do this. Those with high educational attainment tend to be rewarded in the labour market, and thus wealth and educational achievement are positively correlated. In addition, wealth increases with age, as it is accumulated during one's working life. Since

Figure 4.8: Distribution (by decile) and sources of wealth in 2006/8 and 2008/10, £m

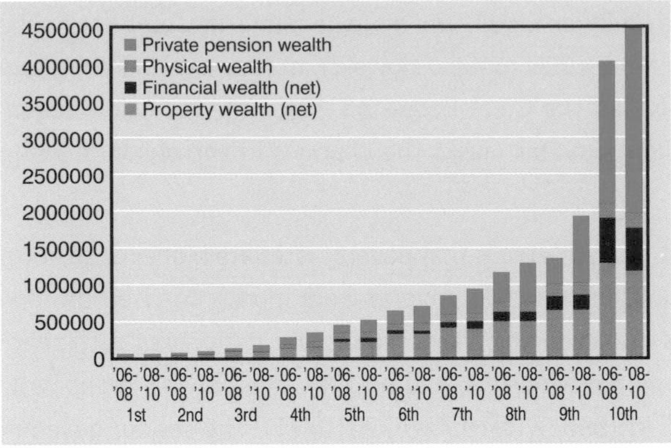

Source: ONS

wealth generates income (e.g. shares pay dividends) wealth inequality is a significant cause of income inequality. Average household wealth has increased considerably over the past 25 years, more than doubling between 1987 and 2009, increasing from £56,000 to £117,000 (at 2008-09 prices). Household wealth fell slightly after 2007 mostly due to a fall in property prices but strong increases in house prices from 2013 onwards has reversed this.

Data for the period 2008-10 shows that the aggregate total household wealth for all households in Great Britain was £10.3 trillion, and the distribution of this wealth is highly uneven. The wealthiest 10% of households were 4.3 times wealthier than the bottom 50% of households combined, and the wealthiest 20% of households owned 62% of aggregate household wealth. The top 1% own around one-fifth of all household wealth in the UK.

Extension material: the inheritance tax debate

Inheritance tax is a hotly debated topic. Inheritance tax is levied at 40% on wealth valued at more than £325,000 (in 2014/15) unless it is left to your spouse. The threshold for married couples and civil partners is £650,000. One of the Conservatives key manifesto promises for the 2010 election was to raise the inheritance tax threshold to £1 million. They claimed that passing on your wealth to family members when you die was a natural instinct, and people should have the right to do so. Others, such as the American billionaire investor Warren Buffet are staunch supporters of high inheritance tax. They argue that inheritance tax is one of the few progressive taxes remaining, and it reduces intergenerational wealth and income inequality. Furthermore, allowing people to inherit large amounts of wealth from their parents discourages work and entrepreneurial activity, and some argue that their high standard of living isn't 'earned'. Buffet has warned that the US is in danger of creating an 'oligarchy' if inheritance tax isn't increased. When the Coalition government was formed in 2010 the Liberal Democrats had their preferred policy implemented of raising the personal allowance on income tax, and the inheritance tax threshold was not raised significantly.

● Knowledge: Poverty definitions

It is hard to say what exactly 'poverty' means, as people's interpretations as to what constitutes poverty are different. However, economists split poverty into two categories.

Absolute poverty is the situation where an individual, household or group struggle to obtain the basic necessities required to sustain human life such as food, water, and clean clothes.

Relative poverty is the situation in which an individual, household or group faces a low material standard of living relative to the rest of society, and are in danger of **social exclusion**. In the UK members of a household are in relative poverty if their household income is less than 60% of the median. This is known as the 'poverty line'.

● ● Application and Analysis: Changes in poverty since 1997

As income inequality increased between 1979 and 1990 the number of households in relative poverty rose significantly, with child poverty increasing three fold during this period. Although the early and mid-1990s saw a stabilising or even a slight reversal in child poverty rates, by 1997, the UK's child poverty rate was amongst the worst of all rich nations with around one in three children living in relative poverty. When

Labour came to power in 1997 they made a concrete pledge to reduce poverty rates, with a particular focus on child poverty. During Labour's first two terms (1997-2005) policies such as the introduction of the Working Families Tax Credit, the Child Tax Credit, and more generous means-tested benefits for pensioners contributed to a fall in poverty rates for all groups. However, during Labour's third term child and overall poverty rates rose until the onset of the Great Recession. Since the recession began in 2008 however, relative poverty rates have fallen, but this masks the changes in the absolute living standards of the poorest (as explained below).

From Tables 4.3 and 4.4 the first thing to note is that poverty rates are higher once housing costs are taken into consideration. Labour's policies to tackle poverty were mostly focused on redistributing income towards pensioners and families with children on low income. One criticism of such policies is that working-age non-parents were ignored by policy makers, and poverty rates for this group rose during the period shown above (from 17.2% AHC in 1996/7 to 19.7% in 2010/11). The Labour government set a target in 1999 to halve child poverty by 2010/11, and eliminate it all together by 2020. By 2010/11, child poverty had only fallen from 4.2m to 3.6m (AHC), missing the target by some margin.

Table 4.3: Relative poverty in the UK: households below 60% of median income (after housing costs, AHC)

	Children (%)	Children (millions)	Pensioners (%)	Pensioners (millions)	All (%)	All (millions)
1996/7	34.1	4.3	29.1	2.9	25.3	14.0
2000/01	31.1	3.9	25.9	2.6	23.1	13.0
2004/5	28.4	3.6	17.6	1.9	20.5	12.1
2007/8	31.1	3.9	18.1	2.0	22.5	13.5
2010/11	27.3	3.6	14.2	1.7	21.3	13.0

Source: Cribb, Joyce & Phillip, *Living Standards, Inequality and Poverty in the UK 2012*, IFS

Table 4.4: Relative poverty in the UK: households below 60% of median income (before housing costs, BHC)

	Children (%)	Children (millions)	Pensioners (%)	Pensioners (millions)	All (%)	All (millions)
1996/7	26.7	3.4	24.6	2.4	19.4	10.8
2000/01	23.3	3.0	24.8	2.5	18.4	10.4
2004/5	21.3	2.7	21.3	2.3	17.0	10.0
2007/8	22.5	2.9	22.7	2.5	18.3	11.0
2010/11	17.5	2.3	17.5	2.0	16.1	9.8

Source: Cribb, Joyce & Phillip, *Living Standards, Inequality and Poverty in the UK 2012*, IFS

The Labour government was unsuccessful in meeting overall and child poverty reduction targets despite increasing average spending per child in the social security system. One of the main reasons poverty reduction did not occur is due to the problem with the relative poverty measure. Despite adopting poverty reduction targets the New Labour government had a very relaxed stance on general levels of inequality, and particularly rapid income growth at the top of the income distribution. Given that the relative poverty line is measured by 60% of median household income, the only way poverty rates can fall is if incomes at the bottom of the distribution grow quicker than those in the middle. As shown in Figure 4.3 the incomes for all 5 quintiles grew at roughly the same rate under Labour, meaning that relative poverty reduction was difficult as the incomes at the bottom did not gain significantly on those in middle of the distribution. Another contributing factor was the system of state benefits being linked to inflation, which was lower than earnings growth throughout the vast majority of Labour's time in office. Therefore, despite rises in absolute living standards for many of those at the bottom end of the income distribution, relative poverty rates remained stubbornly high.

The effects of the 2008-09 recession and subsequent squeeze on household incomes caused a fall in relative poverty rates, as shown in tables 4.3 and 4.4. This may seem counter-intuitive at first. As previously mentioned, since the Great Recession the incomes of those at the bottom of the distribution have been squeezed by less than those at top and the middle of the distribution as shown in Figure 4.5. Therefore, despite falling real incomes across the board, the incomes of the poorest have caught up with the median, thus causing relative poverty rates to fall.

So despite falling living standards at the bottom end of the distribution since the Great Recession, relative poverty rates have fallen. This highlights a key problem with the measure; it tells us little about absolute living standards. In fact, child material deprivation has been rising since the start of the Great Recession, and rose by 300,000 in 2012-13 alone according to the IFS, showing a fall in the absolute living standards of many of the poorest households despite a fall in relative poverty rates.

Another limitation of the relative poverty measure is that it does little to inform us about the living standards of those who are in poverty, and whether their absolute living standards are improving or not. There is some evidence to suggest that the hardship of those in poverty is growing. Despite a general fall in relative poverty since 1997, relative poverty using a threshold of 40% of median income has risen, showing a rise in the proportion of the population who are 'very poor'.

As many planned benefit cuts come into full effect, such as the accelerated cuts to the working-age social security budget from April 2013, the absolute living standards for those at the bottom end of the distribution may well fall. Whether relative poverty rates rise or not depends on how the incomes of other groups alter in coming years.

Question

4. Evaluate the effectiveness of at least three policies which might be used to reduce inequality and eradicate poverty.

●● Knowledge and Application: An economic divide between regions

Overall data on inequality and poverty in the UK hides substantial inequality between regions. Historically Regional Policy has been used to help support less prosperous regions but over time the UK has had to adopt a more 'hands off' approach to comply with EU Regional Policy framework and its strong opposition to 'unfair' competition such as state aid. Two remaining initiatives with regional dimensions include:

● The Selective Finance for Investment in England and Scotland program – offers grants to support start-ups, business expansion, innovation and R&D.

● The European Regional Development Fund.

Figure 4.9 shows the considerable variation in weekly earnings between regions, with weekly earnings in London being 35% higher than those in the North East. Also, the data shows something of a North-South divide. The only three regions whose median weekly earnings exceeded that of the UK average were London, East of England and the South-East.

Between 2000 and 2007 many of the less prosperous regions such as the North East started to close the gap as they experienced significant falls in unemployment and rises in house prices. During and after the 2008-09 recession however, Northern Regions suffered more from rising unemployment and house price falls, while property in London and the South-East maintained value better. Furthermore, the local economies of several 'outer' regions such as the North-East and Wales have become very dependent upon the public sector. The Coalition's spending and public sector jobs cuts (amounting to 180,000 between 2010 and 2013) have hit those regions the hardest, and the North-South divide appears to be getting larger once again.

Figure 4.9: Regional differences in median gross weekly earnings

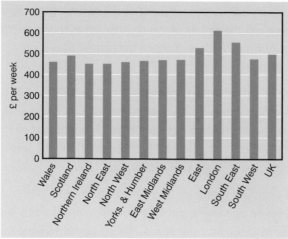

Source: ONS *Region and Country Profile*, 2012

Figure 4.10: Average house price by country and region in 2012

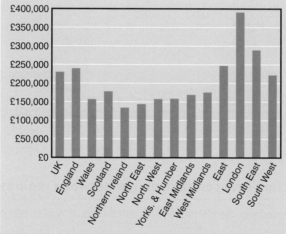

Source: ONS House Price survey

Figures 4.9 and 4.10 show much higher levels of earnings and house prices in London than other regions. This has led some economists to point to a London – other regions divide, rather than a North – South divide. However, the London economy is not without its problems. As shown in Table 4.5 unemployment and inactivity rates are above the national average. High house prices have made many dependent upon housing benefit. Obtaining work or more work would mean this important source of income would be lost, creating a large disincentive. Furthermore, the absence of a London minimum wage further reduces the incentive to work. Child poverty is also a major problem in London. The campaign group End Child Poverty estimate that 1 in 4 children in London live in poverty, compared to 1 in 5 nationally. The borough of Tower Hamlets has the highest child poverty level in the UK, at 52%. This highlights a key point of note; there is as much of a divide *within* regions as there is *between* regions.

Table 4.5: Unemployment and inactivity rates by region

	Unemployment rate (%)	Inactivity rates (%)		Unemployment rate (%)	Inactivity rates (%)
United Kingdom	8.3	23.3	East Midlands	8.0	21.9
Wales	9.3	25.3	West Midlands	8.9	25.5
Scotland	8.0	22.5	East	6.9	20.2
Northern Ireland	7.3	27.1	London	9.7	24.7
North East	11.6	26.4	South East	6.3	20.8
North West	8.5	24.7	South West	6.6	20.9
Yorks and Humber	10.3	24.6			

Source: ONS *Region and Country Profile*, 2012

Chapter 5

UK Trade, the Current Account and the Value of the Pound

This chapter examines the position of, and recent changes in, the different components of the current account on the balance of payments. The significance of the UK's persistent current account deficit is then discussed. Finally, the chapter identifies recent changes in the external value of the pound sterling, the causes of these changes and their importance.

● Knowledge: **The meaning of the current account**

There are three components of the Balance of Payments: The Current Account, the Financial Account and the Capital Account. The most important component of which is the current account balance, which this chapter will focus upon.

In short, the current account measures flows of income into and out of the economy. Each section is itself a 'balance', i.e. it takes into account both inflows and outflows. The current account contains four sections:

1. The **balance of trade in goods**: such as automobiles, pharmaceuticals, agricultural products and oil, calculated by value of exported goods minus value of goods imported.

2. The **balance of trade in services**: such as financial services, shipping and tourism, calculated by value of exported services minus value of services imported.

3. The **income balance**: the balance of factor income i.e. net income from employing factors of production. This could include interest from loans made, dividends from shares purchased, profits from a company's operations, or remittances sent to family members. So, if a UK company makes a profit on an overseas operation, there will be an inflow of income to the UK thus improving the income balance. If a Polish worker in the UK sends some of their earnings back to their family in Poland, this represents an outflow of income which will worsen the income balance.

4. **Net transfers** include central government transfers to international organisations such as the IMF, UN and EU, as well as foreign aid.

Questions

1. What is the different between the budget balance and the current account balance?

2. For each of the following scenarios, identify which section of the current account is affected, and whether an inflow or outflow occurs. Also comment on whether the current account improves or worsens as a result.

   (a) Cars from the Nissan factory in Sunderland are sold to a French car retailer for sale in France.

   (b) The UK government increases its development aid spending.

   (c) Barclays receives repayments (with the agreed rate of interest) from a Swedish company.

   (d) A British manufacturer hires a Dutch company to audit their company accounts.

● Application: **The state of the current account in 2011**

Achieving a surplus on the current account balance was a major macroeconomic policy objective of the UK government for much of the post-war era. Governments believed that in order to buy goods and services from the rest of the world you must export at least as many goods and services or you would be unable to obtain the necessary foreign currency to import without selling off foreign assets, or accumulate excessive

Table 5.1: Summary of the UK current account balance in 2012

	£m
Exports of goods	299,500
Imports of goods	407,400
Exports of services	193,400
Imports of services	119,400
Balance of trade in goods and services	-33,900
Income balance	-2,100
Net transfers	-23,100
Current Account Balance	**-59,200**

Source: ONS, *UK Pink Book 2013*

Figure 5.1: Current account balance and balance as a percentage of GDP

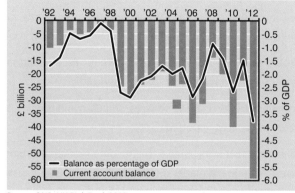

Source: ONS, *UK Pink Book 2013*

Figure 5.2: Trade in goods and services

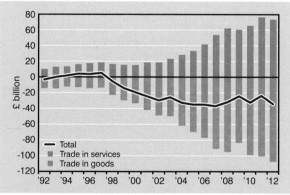

Source: ONS, *UK Pink Book 2013*

Figure 5.3: Top 10 UK export destinations

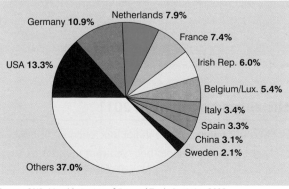

Source: ONS, *Monthly Review of External Trade Statistics*, 2012

levels of debt. From the mid-1980s, however, a combination of the City of London drawing in vast amounts of foreign capital, the evolution of a more complex financial system and more relaxed attitude to debt meant that the current account balance became less important as a macroeconomic policy objective. The UK has had a current account deficit every year since 1984. Since the financial crisis of 2008, however, the view that a persistent current account deficit is unsustainable in the long run has become popular once again. Table 5.1 shows that the UK economy has a significant current account deficit, caused primarily by a large trade in goods deficit.

Trade is of vital importance to the UK economy. The UK has a long history of supporting free trade and remains one of the most open advanced economies. The value of exports and imports were slightly above 30% of GDP in 2012. The UK is the world's second largest exporter of services and has run a balance of trade in services surplus since 1966. However, the UK has experienced a prolonged decline in competitiveness for exporting goods, leading to a record trade in goods deficit in 2012 of £107.9bn.

Figure 5.2 shows that over the last 20 years the trade in services surplus has grown while the trade in goods deficit has worsened. For the period shown the trade in goods deficit has worsened more quickly than the trade in services surplus has improved, causing the overall trade balance to fall deeper into deficit.

Despite globalisation, the majority of the UK's trade is done with her neighbours. The EU accounted for 53.2% of the UK's exports and 49.29% of imports in 2012. The amount of trade between the UK and the EU has risen considerably since the UK joined in 1973, but the US, the world's largest economy, remains the largest buyer of UK exports. Most EU countries have experienced sluggish growth in recent years, particularly since the financial crisis of 2008, and the subsequent Eurozone debt crisis. This dashed hopes that the depreciation of sterling in 2007 could bring

Figure 5.4: Top 10 UK import sources

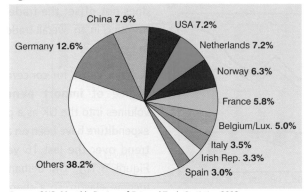

Source: ONS, *Monthly Review of External Trade Statistics*, 2012

Figure 5.5: Top 10 UK exports by commodity (£m)

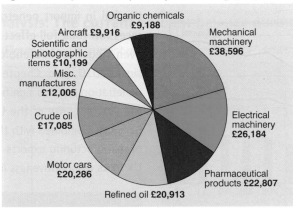

Source: ONS, *Monthly Review of External Trade Statistics*, 2012

Figure 5.6: Top 10 UK imports by commodity (£m)

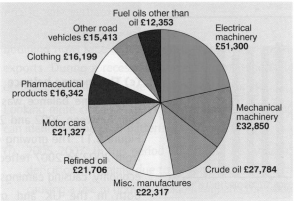

Source: ONS, *Monthly Review of External Trade Statistics*, 2012

Figure 5.7: Trade in goods

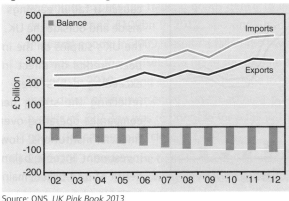

Source: ONS, *UK Pink Book 2013*

an export-led recovery. Furthermore, most economists agree that the UK needs to re-orient exports towards faster growing emerging markets, as Germany has done. Imports to the UK from emerging economies have risen considerably in recent years, with China now being the second largest source of imports as shown in Figure 5.4. Therefore, most economists agree that the UK needs to rebalance its trade with these economies by exporting more to them, though progress in this area remains slow.

(a) The balance of trade in goods

Figures 5.5 and 5.6 show that the UK trades similar items with the rest of the World. The most important traded items for the UK are mechanical machinery, oil (crude and refined), electrical machinery and pharma-ceuticals. The UK has traditionally run a trade in goods deficit, and the last 10 years has been no exception, as shown in Figure 5.7. Although the value of exports has grown, reaching a record high in 2012, the value of imports has risen by more, hence the record goods deficit in that year.

Since the discovery of North Sea oil in the 1980s, net exports of this commodity, as well as natural gas, prevented trade in goods from going further into deficit. Since 2005 however, the UK has run a deficit on its trade in oil balance, as shown in Figure 5.8. The deficit on trade in oil is set to grow as stocks decline over the next decade, with an estimated fall in output of 6% per annum.

(b) UK balance of trade in services

The UK has run a trade in services surplus every year since 1966. This is mainly because the UK has a **comparative advantage** in services, with financial services playing an especially important role, accounting for around 25% of UK service exports. The English language also makes exports of other professional services such as consultancy and advertising competitive. However, services are not as tradable as goods, and there are greater legal and language barriers for trading services internationally. As a result the value of trade in services is less than that

supply and demand for the pound. The exchange rate appreciated between 1996 and 2001, and then remained broadly constant until 2006, when the value of the pound rose again. The exchange rate fell dramatically, by almost 30% between late 2007 and early 2009. Since then, the pound has gradually appreciated against other major currencies.

The reasons for these changes are outlined below:

1996-late 2007: During this period the pound was generally strengthening or remaining at a high level. This was due to:

● Confidence in the UK economic growth and macroeconomic policy framework leading to speculative buying of pounds.

● During this period the Bank of England had higher interest rates than the ECB, Bank of Japan, and at times, the Federal reserve. This led to an inflow of **hot money**.

● The City of London attracted vast inflows of FDI during this period, raising demand for pounds.

● The US trade deficit weakened the dollar, which boosted sterling's trade weighted exchange rate.

Late 2007-mid 2009: The value of the pound plummeted during this period due to:

● A deep recession in the UK reduced confidence in the UK economy, causing speculators to sell pounds.

● The 2008 financial crisis hit the City of London especially hard, halting FDI and portfolio investment flows into the UK.

● Between July 2007 and March 2009 the base rate of interest set by the Bank of England was cut from 5.75% to 0.5%, where it has remained. This caused a hot money outflow.

● A return to a more realistic value against the euro and the dollar was likely to happen sooner or later, and this adjustment occurred as a result of the financial crisis.

Mid 2009-2014: The value of the pound has slowly appreciated due to:

● The pound appreciated against the dollar from a low of £1 = $1.38 in March 2009, but the main reason for the rising value of sterling has been the appreciation of the pound against the euro since 2010, which is given more importance on the trade weighted index as over 40% of the UK's trade is with the Eurozone. This has been due to the Eurozone debt crisis lowering confidence in Eurozone economies. Fears of a currency area break up has caused financial capital to move from the Eurozone to the UK, which is seen as a relatively safe haven. As the recovery finally took hold from Q1 2013 to mid-2014, with annualised quarterly growth rates between 2% and 4%, confidence in the UK economy grew, attracting speculation to buy pounds.

Despite the recent gradual strengthening of the pound since mid-2009, its value remains well below the level experienced at the end of the NICE decade. The consequences of having a weaker pound are:

● An improvement in export competitiveness.

● A potential (and as yet unseen) decrease in import penetration as the price of imports rises, making domestically produced goods relatively cheaper.

● A rise in inflation as the cost of essential imports such as food, energy and clothing increase. Also, imported raw material costs rise for domestic firms.

● Potentially, an export-led recovery as foreigners take advantage of cheaper goods and services produced in the UK, and UK consumers reduce the amount they purchase from overseas. However, as mentioned before, there is little evidence such an effect has taken place so far.

● Potentially higher profits for UK companies operating overseas, as their overseas earnings are more valuable in pound terms. This could improve the income surplus.

Question

6. To what extent will a fall in the value of the pound improve UK macroeconomic performance?

Chapter 6
The Supply Side: Productivity and Competitiveness

This chapter examines how the UK economy has performed in terms of productivity growth and why this is an important issue. Measures to raise productivity are considered in the context of diminished competitiveness of UK firms relative to some other developed countries.

●● Knowledge and Application: What is productivity?

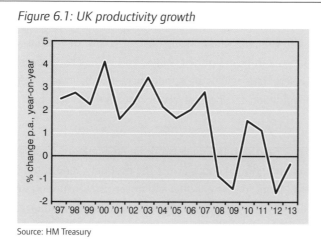
Figure 6.1: UK productivity growth

Source: HM Treasury

Productivity measures the ratio of output to input, in other words the production of goods and services as a proportion of the factors of production used to make them. Although productivity can be measured for all factors of production, it is **labour productivity** which is of most concern to macroeconomists. **Labour productivity** is the ratio of output to labour input, typically measured as the total value of output (GDP) per hour worked. Using 'hours worked' rather than the employment level adjusts the data for part-time work and overtime.

Figure 6.1 shows that for much of the period 1997-2007 the UK experienced productivity growth averaging the long-run trend rate of economic growth of 2.5%. However, productivity growth fell during the recession of 2008-09 and again in 2012 and 2013.

● Analysis: What drives increases in productivity?

Productivity growth is a key measure of macroeconomic performance. It refers to the increase over time in the productive capacity of the macroeconomy and, therefore, drives long-run, or trend growth. We can identify a number of the determinants of labour productivity:

1. Investment in human capital
Highly-skilled and trained workers are more productive as they can produce more output in a given period of time, with less waste. Better management can also motivate workers to be more productive, and organise resources better so workers can focus on core performance. Education and training are fundamentally important in creating workers with relevant and transferable skills, and good healthcare can also boost labour productivity by keeping workers healthy and reducing the number of working days lost to illness.

2. Investment in physical capital
Fixed capital investment – spending by firms on ICT and up-to-date technologies and machinery – boosts labour productivity in two ways. Firstly, it allows some replacement of labour by capital in tasks where a machine or robot is more efficient and accurate, for example in some manufacturing tasks such as car production. Secondly, better equipment can increase the productivity of remaining workers by allowing them to better organise their time or to perform manufacturing tasks.

3. Financial capital
If investment drives productivity gains, it is crucial that firms of all sizes have access to affordable credit. This allows them to invest in the latest technologies and match competition in both domestic and

international markets. The credit crisis in 2007 and its lasting impact on capital markets can be seen as one cause of the UK's 'productivity gap' (see later in the chapter).

4. Product market competition

The more firms there are competing in a market, the more likely they are forced to compete on both prices and costs. Labour costs contribute a significant proportion to total costs in most modern organisations, and therefore firms will work hard to keep unit labour costs as low as possible. The key here is labour productivity: highly-skilled workers are valuable even if their wages are higher than other workers, as their higher cost is offset (and probably outweighed) by their increased output levels.

5. Labour market competition

The negotiating power of workers is an important determinant of labour productivity. Where workers enjoy considerable bargaining power (for example when unemployment is low, or when a worker has skills in shortage in the labour market) they can push up their wages. This will increase their employer's labour costs. Similarly, in an economy where trade unions are strong there may be lower productivity levels, and policies such as minimum wage legislation can increase labour costs in the lowest-paid jobs.

6. Infrastructure

Infrastructure refers to the transport and distribution networks in an economy. Good infrastructure eases the flow of workers, raw materials and finished goods across the economy, reducing the labour hours lost to unpredictable commuting travel times, delays and fuel and driver costs incurred as output is delivered to markets. Both internal and external transport links are crucial in keeping distribution costs to a minimum, and in making the UK an attractive place to do business and attract foreign direct investment.

7. Government policies

Many of the factors already raised can be influenced by government intervention (or lack of intervention) in the markets for raw materials, financial capital, labour and transport. Research and development (R&D) spending can also be targeted through the use of tax breaks and subsidies.

● Analysis: **Why is productivity growth important?**

Productivity growth is important for a number of reasons:

1. Productivity growth improves living standards by increasing the level of output relative to the size of the population. This helps to explain why real incomes and real output tend to increase over time, and why each generation enjoys a wider and more affordable range of goods and services than the generation before. Productivity gains boost output per worker, and also reflect the adoption of new innovations and inventions which increase quality of life as well as standard of living.

2. Increases in productivity increase output through supply-side improvements, rather than higher aggregate demand. As long-run aggregate supply rises, output and employment levels rise without pushing up prices; indeed, the price of some goods and services may fall as their unit costs fall. Non-inflationary growth does not carry the same trade-off between output and inflationary pressures, and thus is seen as highly beneficial for (nearly) all economic agents.

3. Labour productivity is a key factor in determining international competitiveness: the ability of an economy such as the UK to produce the goods and services demanded by global consumers, firms and governments. **Unit labour costs** are a key performance measure, and are calculated by dividing average wages by average output. If the UK is able to compete strongly in international markets it will experience demand for its exports. This will avoid problems with current account imbalance and create jobs for UK-based workers and profits for UK-based firms, rather than those in other countries.

4. Finally, productivity growth can be a sign of other strengths. If labour costs are low relative to output, this can reflect an economy with well-trained, organised and motivated workers. High levels of

investment create both demand and future supply, and the incomes and profits created by economic activity will boost government's tax receipts. A strong infrastructure improves quality of life as well as keeping firms' costs low.

There are possible drawbacks to strong labour productivity growth, the main one being **structural unemployment**. This exists when the unemployed (those *seeking work*) do not have the relevant skills for the vacancies available (the firms *seeking workers*). Structural unemployment is often linked closely to shifts in technology and patterns of global production, and is most likely where workers have specific and non-transferable skills related to industries which move overseas to take advantage of cheaper labour and land (see Chapter 7).

Question

1. Paul Krugman has said that "productivity isn't everything, but in the long run it is almost everything."[1] Why is it arguable that productivity growth is, in the ultimate, the key indicator of a country's standard of living?

● **Application: UK versus global productivity performance**

Figure 6.2: Average productivity growth for selected G7 members, 1997-2007 and 1997-2011

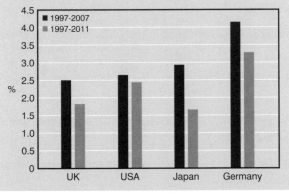

Source: HM Treasury

Figure 6.3: Highest annual increase in productivity, 1997-2007

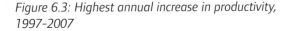

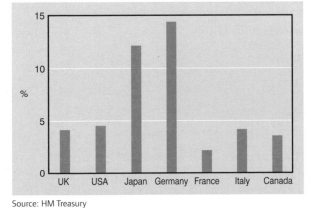

Source: HM Treasury

Figure 6.2 shows how average UK productivity growth compared with other major economies over two time periods. For the period 1997-2007 the UK experienced a growing gap in productivity against the USA, Japan and Germany. A similar trend is shown for 1997-2011, where a dramatic fall in productivity in 2009 (-14.8%) dragged down the Japan average. For the G7 economies, the highest annual increase in productivity recorded since 1997 is shown in Figure 6.3. Even in its best year the UK did not perform well compared with several other developed economies.

As seen in Figure 6.4, the UK and USA have invested a lower proportion of GDP than Germany and Japan in recent years, and their productivity growth has been lower as a result. However, other economies such as France and Italy have also suffered low productivity growth despite proportionately higher levels of investment.

1. P. Krugman, *The Age of Diminished Expectations*, 1999.

Figure 6.4: Investment as % of GDP (2001-11 average) for G7 economies

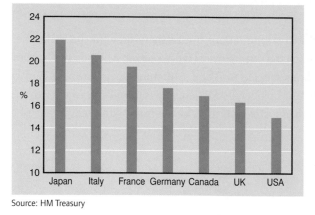

Source: HM Treasury

Question

2. Figure 6.4 shows that Italy and Japan both devoted over 20% of their GDP to investment but in Figure 6.3 the two countries differed in their experience in productivity growth. How could one explain this difference?

● Analysis: **The UK productivity gap**

The term 'productivity gap' has been used in recent years to describe the loss of competitiveness of UK firms against those in similar economies. It is a key factor in the debate surrounding deindustrialisation (see Chapter 3, and Figure 3.3 in particular) and is often given as a cause of the relatively low rate of trend economic growth experienced in the UK.

A study by the London School of Economics' Centre for Economic Performance[2] identified the following key aspects of the UK productivity gap:

● Output per hour worked was almost 40% lower than in the USA and 20% lower than in Germany and France.

● Output per worker was similar in the UK and Germany, but UK labour works 16% higher hours than in Germany.

● The key factors explaining the productivity gap between the UK and France and Germany are lower capital invested per worker and lower skills.

● The productivity gap between the UK and USA is most acute in three sectors: wholesale and retailing, hotels and restaurants, and financial services.

● The productivity gap between the UK and USA was caused less by a lack of investment in labour and capital, and more by differences in managerial methods and technology.

Since 2004, the productivity gap has remained.

Table 6.1: Changes in UK productivity, 2003-12

Output per worker	7.3%
Output per job	7.4%
Output per hour	9.4%
Unit labour costs	22.9%

Source: ONS

Table 6.1 shows how although UK output has increased since 2003, in particular in terms of output per hour, unit labour costs have risen by almost a quarter over the period. Between 2006 and 2010 the UK-USA productivity gap increased by 9%, with US productivity per hour 23% higher than in the UK. Similar gaps of 18% and 16% were recorded between the UK and Germany and France respectively. Figure 6.5 compares growth in unit labour costs with other G7 economies and the eurozone average.

---

2. http://www2.lse.ac.uk/newsAndMedia/news/archives/2004/UKs_ProductivityGap.aspx

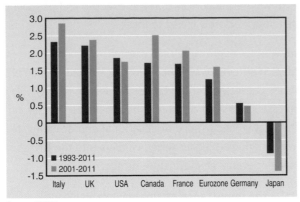

Figure 6.5: Average growth in unit labour costs, 1993-2011 and 2001-11

Source: HM Treasury

Figure 6.6: Sterling effective exchange rate index (January 2005 = 100)

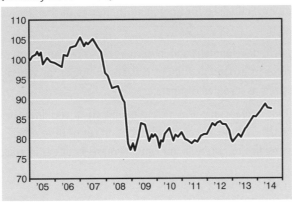

Source: Bank of England

The UK and Italy clearly saw unit labour costs in their manufacturing sectors increase by more than the G7 and eurozone averages. In comparison, Japan saw its labour costs fall over both periods, and Germany enjoyed wage inflation of less than 1% compared to output levels.

It should be noted that this data reflects the strength of domestic currencies, or in the case of Germany, Italy and France, the strength of the euro. A stronger, or appreciating currency increases the prices of domestically-produced goods and services in overseas markets; a depreciating currency reduces the prices of domestic outputs overseas.

The relatively strong pound during 'the NICE decade' therefore could go some way in explaining comparatively poor unit labour costs, but would not explain the 'real' gap in output per hour and output per worker. Figure 6.6 shows the sterling effective exchange rate index between 2003 and 2012. This is a trade-weighted average, and therefore reflects the relative importance of different currencies. Throughout 2003 to 2008, the index remained high, but the fall in sterling throughout 2008 should have increased UK productivity relative to other major trading partners.

● Analysis: The 'productivity puzzle'

The trends in employment, unemployment and productivity levels in the UK in recent months has given rise to the term 'productivity puzzle.' With output contracting (falling real GDP in the double dip recession), economists would expect to see unemployment rising and employment falling. However, in the final months of 2012 the UK saw rising employment and falling unemployment. The impact of this on UK productivity is clear: more workers producing fewer goods and services implies a fall in output per worker. This is explored further in Chapter 7, where the main causes suggested are 'labour hoarding', a collapse in investment, and falling real wages.

As discussed earlier in the chapter, UK productivity has declined in recent years despite rising real GDP and record levels of employment. This supports a view of the UK economy that much of the job creation has been in low skill work and demand is supported by imports and a wealth effect from rising property prices, predominantly in the more prosperous regions of the UK.

Questions

3. Why would you expect labour hoarding by employers to have an adverse effect on productivity?

4. If interest rates are very low why nonetheless might employers be reluctant to install new capital equipment?

● ● Analysis and Evaluation: Minding the gap – policies to boost productivity

The causes of productivity growth were explored earlier in this chapter, and possible policies to increase productivity performance will therefore be closely linked to these.

1. Investing in human capital

Recent governments have stressed, in different ways, the importance of creating an efficient, competitive workforce with the skills and abilities necessary for the UK to compete in increasingly globalised product markets. A key debate is to what extent skills can and should be developed through private firms and free markets, or by government. The relative importance of vocational and academic skills is also open to argument. Immigration is one way of bringing higher skilled workers into the UK labour market, but this can also lead to higher unemployment even if employment is rising.

2. Investing in physical capital – the importance of financial capital

Trends in investment spending are covered in greater detail in Chapter 3, but a key determinant is the cost and availability of finance. Again, the debate hinges on whether greater government intervention will increase or decrease the cost of loans to firms. Banks were criticised during the credit crisis for easy lending during the NICE decade, and are now criticised for tightening the terms of their lending as the economy struggles to recover from recession.

In addition, the reward for research, development and investment is important: high rates of corporation tax can limit the incentive for firms to expand and adopt new technologies, as well as reducing post-tax profits which are used by some firms as a source of finance.

Free market economists argue that bureaucracy also increases unit costs and limits innovation by raising the cost of doing business in the UK. They would also argue that, in terms of research, governments have a habit of 'backing losers' and subsidies to potential innovators create a culture of state dependency with low incentives for success.

3. Increasing product market competition

This is seen by many economists as the key driver of innovation, investment and rising productivity. Globalisation and free trade expose UK firms to powerful market trends, forcing them to control their costs to compete. However, this has also led to the loss of jobs to overseas producers and production plants, with structural unemployment resulting in the UK.

4. Increasing labour market competition

The 'labour hoarding' argument given for the productivity puzzle suggests that UK labour markets may not be as flexible as expected. If firms are holding on to workers despite falling demand, this suggests the costs of redundancy are high and there may be a shortage of sufficiently skilled workers when the economy recovers.

Labour market imperfections such as the National Minimum Wage may also raise labour costs and reduce productivity, but such initiatives play an important role in creating social welfare and reducing poverty and inequality.

5. Investing in infrastructure

Large scale investment projects such as new runways (or even airports) and spending on public transport can boost both short-run growth (through Keynesian-style expansion and related multiplier and accelerator effects) and long-run growth (through reducing transport costs and increasing production and distribution potential).

The UK road, rail and airport network is seriously congested, particularly around major population areas such as London and the north-west conurbation of Manchester and Liverpool.

However, public spending is currently limited by the Coalition government's austerity measures, which aim to bring down public spending as a proportion of GDP to allow greater free market activity.

At least until 2015 (and possibly later given the Labour Party's agreement on the need to cut the budget deficit, albeit over a slightly longer time scale) it appears unlikely that the UK will see a 1930s-style public spending stimulus in an attempt to boost growth, create jobs and ultimately raise productivity.

● ● Knowledge **and** Application: **UK Competition Policy**

The competitiveness of British business is a key driver of innovation, productivity and the efficient functioning of the modern economy. These factors in turn drive improvements in GDP and the external trade balance.

A reduction in the number of competitors can lead to firms then failing to reduce their prices when they have the opportunity to do so, because they know that such a reduction would quickly be matched by their competitors. No communication between firms is necessary and this behaviour is known as tacit collusion, leading to prices which are 'sticky downwards'.

Although much economic analysis focuses on the price effects of ineffective competition, it is important to note that evidence of inefficient competition can also, or instead, emerge in the form of lower quality, a reduced range of goods and services, and/or poorer service. Competition analysts accordingly look at the price, quality, range, service combination (PQRS) rather than focusing on price alone. Also, inefficient competition does not necessarily lead to high profits. Firms that have little to fear from competition are often inefficient, so their higher prices are eaten into by their high cost base, often including higher wages.

Competition is such an important driver of economic performance that most countries in the world, including all countries in the European Union, have created competition authorities with strong legal powers aimed at preserving or increasing the extent of competition within their borders. From 1st April 2014 the **Competition Commission (CC)** and **Office of Fair Trading (OFT)** were combined in the UK into the **Competition and Markets Authority (CMA)**. These competition powers fall into five categories.

1. **Merger Control** aims to prevent firms gaining market power as a result of acquiring control of competitors. In the UK, the CMA reviews all significant mergers with a view to prohibiting those that are likely to result in a **substantial lessening of competition**. Smaller mergers are exempt from scrutiny – i.e. if the turnover of the firm being taken over is £70m or less *and* the combined firms will have no more than 25% market share. But mergers that create a company with a combined market share of more than 25% are very often allowed as long as the market remains competitive and/or it is relatively easy for new firms to enter the market.

2. It can be harder to counter the effects of market power if it arises otherwise than as a result of a merger. In the UK, however, the CMA has the ability to undertake **Market Investigations** of sectors in which there is evidence of inadequate competition. The CMA looks to see if it can identify an **adverse effect on competition** (AEC) arising out of identifiable features of the market. If so, the CMA has extensive powers to remedy the AEC by imposing behavioural conditions or forcing companies to sell part of their business. These very strong powers are in practice used quite rarely, but they can be valuable where a market appears to be working very badly, or where privatisation has created a company with very strong market power.

3. But most countries, including the UK, have **Economic Regulators** which act as a substitute for competition where companies have **substantial market power** (SMP), most obviously where there is a natural monopoly, for instance in **the utility industries** where companies often have **a natural monopoly** in supplying energy, water etc. via wires and pipes which are expensive to duplicate. These companies may only operate if licensed to do so by the regulator, which will impose strict limits on the extent to which the company may raise prices or reduce the quality and range of its products, or the quality of its customer service. Examples of regulatory bodies in the UK are the Office for the Gas and Electricity Markets (OFGEM), water suppliers (OFWAT), the communications sector (OFCOM), railway services (ORR), air traffic services (CAA) and the NHS (Monitor).

● Some people are ineligible for JSA, for example those who have not built up sufficient National Insurance contributions in the past, or those who are not EU citizens.

● People who have left their previous job voluntarily or been dismissed for misconduct are ineligible for JSA.

● Some people may be too embarrassed to claim benefit, or do not understand that they may do so.

It is important to note that where benefit is claimed fraudulently this will increase 'unemployment' on the claimant count measure.

2. The **Labour Force Survey (LFS)** measures unemployment by conducting **a sample survey of over 60,000 households (and over 100,000 people) every three months**. This is the government's official preferred measure of unemployment and compares directly to data collected from all countries according to the International Labour Organisation (ILO). The LFS measure therefore allows economists to judge UK economic performance in the labour market against other economies.

The LFS categorises an individual as unemployed if they:

● Out of work.

● Actively seeking work.

● Been looking for work in the past four weeks.

● Are able to start work within two weeks.

● Application: **UK unemployment data**

Figures 7.1 and 7.2 show the unemployment story for the UK economy over the past 15 years. Figure 7.1 compares Claimant Count and Labour Force Survey levels of unemployment; Figure 7.2 compares the rates of unemployment.

Figure 7.1: Labour Force Survey and Claimant Count unemployment, UK

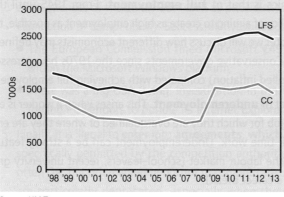

Source: HM Treasury

Figure 7.2: Labour Force Survey and Claimant Count unemployment, UK

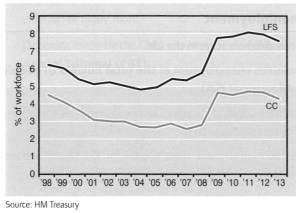

Source: HM Treasury

● Analysis: **Why do the two measures of unemployment differ so much?**

The claimant count is consistently below the Labour Force Survey measure, supporting the view that the former understates unemployment. However, the differential between the measures varies, as shown in Figure 7.3, where data prior to 1998 has also been included to allow for more detailed analysis.

It is very evident that the difference between the LFS and the Claimant Count has increased over the period shown. Possible explanations for the growing divergence between the two measures are:

● Increasing benefit ineligibility (see section on Measuring Unemployment above).

● The impact of long-term unemployment on job seeking; workers who remain jobless for a long period of time may become discouraged to search any longer, or reach retirement age, and therefore stop actively seeking work.

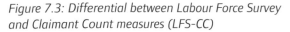

Figure 7.3: Differential between Labour Force Survey and Claimant Count measures (LFS-CC)

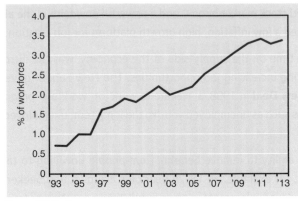

Source: HM Treasury

Figure 7.4: Claimant Count as a percentage of Labour Force Survey, UK

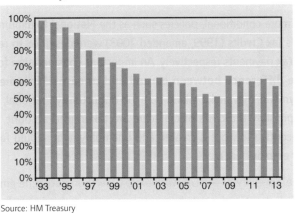

Source: HM Treasury

- The LFS measures members of households who may not be actively seeking work but would accept a job if available, for example parents considering a return to the workforce after taking time to raise a family.

- The stigma associated with 'benefits culture' may prevent some groups such as early retirees from claiming benefits even though they might like to find full-time work in another career or on a part-time basis to supplement income from pensions.

- Increased unemployment of higher earners (perhaps linked to increased incomes in general) which allows workers who have been made redundant to survive on savings and termination packages whilst they look for work.

Figure 7.4 shows how the CC consistently fell relative to the LFS measure between 1993 and 2008, followed by a sharp uplift during and after the recession of 2008-09. It can be argued that, during a recession, the Claimant Count increases because as major earners are made redundant, other possible earners will also become eligible for benefits.

● Analysis: Causes of unemployment in the UK economy

The relationship between unemployment and economic growth is important. Both demand and supply-side factors influence the rates of job creation and job destruction across the economy. It should be noted that new employment opportunities arise even during periods of local and national decline, and there may be job losses and even the collapse of some sectors even when the economy is experiencing a boom.

The difference between those jobs created and those lost will therefore determine the net impact on unemployment in a region or across the United Kingdom.

A key issue in labour markets in rapidly evolving and changing economies is that of the mismatch between the skills of workers losing their jobs and those needed to be successful in finding work in sectors and roles where there are vacancies.

As seen on Figures 7.1, 7.2 and 7.3, UK unemployment has varied widely even over the relatively short period of the past 20 years. Those years can be divided into the following periods:

1993-2004: Stable economic growth
Unemployment fell consistently over this period, with the Labour Force Survey measure in 2004 at less than half of that recorded in 1993 as the economy began its recovery from recession.

The major downward driver of unemployment was, of course, strong and stable economic growth. The departure of sterling from the Exchange Rate Mechanism in 1992 effectively devalued the pound by around 15% against the other major European economies, allowing an export-led boom to create demand

Figure 7.9: Long-term (25 years old +, >12 months unemployment) and Youth (18-24, >6 months unemployment) unemployment in the UK

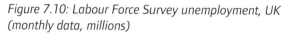
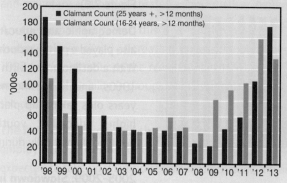

Source: HM Treasury

Question

1. How does the data in Figures 7.7 and 7.9 illustrate the concern over the phenomenon of the Neets?

Figure 7.10: Labour Force Survey unemployment, UK (monthly data, millions)

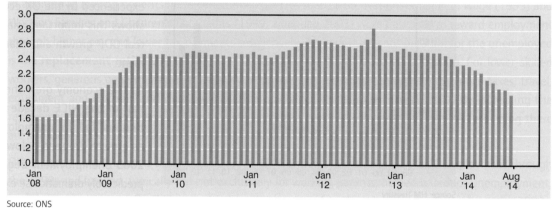

Source: ONS

2009 onwards

Figure 7.10 shows how UK unemployment rose throughout the recession of 2008-09, albeit with a time lag of a few months. Between mid-2008 and mid-2009, the LFS measure recorded an increase in joblessness of 1 million. Even when the economy returned to slow growth in 2010, unemployment remained high around the 2.6 million level.

Declining productivity when GDP growth declines can be explained by factors such as:

Figure 7.11: Annual change in output per worker, UK, 2005-13

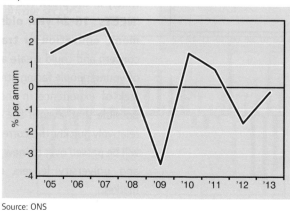

Source: ONS

- 'Labour hoarding': businesses hold onto workers because they are expecting the economy to return to stronger growth imminently and they wish to avoid the costs associated with making redundancies and then re-hiring high quality workers. This can be a positive sign for the macroeconomy.

- Collapse in investment due to the banking crisis: if firms are finding cheap credit difficult to obtain, this will have hindered investment in capital which can boost labour productivity. This links to the third point, below:

- Falling real wages: a combination of a squeezed labour market and relatively high inflation has made hiring or retaining workers a more cost-effective solution than investing in more efficient technologies and capital.

- 'Zombie firms': this argument is that there are firms in the UK which remain in existence despite very low levels of output and investment. These firms are able to meet their debt repayments only because of very low interest rates, and they are not creating surplus profit required to fund investment programmes.

As the economy has continued to recover in 2013 and 2014 there has been an *increase in employment* even during a period where unemployment has been high.

Since February 2012 at least 50,000 jobs have been created in the UK labour market each month, considerably outweighing the increase in unemployment. Therefore rising unemployment *and* employment have to be seen in the context of a growing workforce.

Returning to the issue of long-term and youth unemployed, the latest data (Q3 2014) shows that just under 300,000 people are classified as being unemployed for more than 12 months, with 37,000 of these aged 18-24. Half a million 16-24 year olds are unemployed according to the LFS measure with a clear gender divide in evidence (313,000 men and 191,000 women).

●● Application and Analysis: Unemployment and Recession

The recent recession in 2008-09 illustrates the strong correlation between negative economic growth and increased unemployment. Figure 7.8 shows this relationship earlier in the chapter. In late 2014, UK claimant count was approximately 1 million, of which 0.62 million were men. Factors accounting for this imbalance are:

- Continued job losses in the manufacturing sector due to industrialisation, which has traditionally employed a higher proportion of men than women.

- Lower participation rates of women in the workforce, particularly in the older age groups.

- Under the Labour government of recent years there was an increase in public sector employment which created more jobs, particularly for women.

The main solution to demand-deficient unemployment is to return the macroeconomy to strong growth. The prospect of a continued recovery in the years ahead are discussed elsewhere in the book, but just as the pattern of unemployment is currently asymmetrical, it is likely that future trends in employment and unemployment will affect some groups and regions of the UK more favourably than others.

Figure 7.12: Unemployment by region (% of workforce, September 2012)

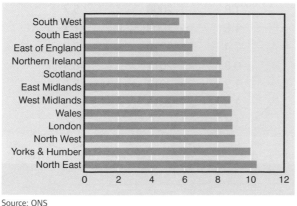

Source: ONS

Areas of key concern are:

- The impact of public sector employment reductions on regions outside London and the south-east; these are areas where the highest levels of public sector job creation occurred.

- The impact of public sector employment reductions on women; by some estimates, the proportion of female employment in the public sector increased at three times the rate of male employment between 2000 and 2010.

Which of the PIIGS has experienced the most dramatic increase in unemployment since 2005?

Figure 7.15: PIIGS unemployment (% of workforce, ILO measure)

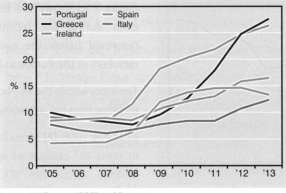

Source: HM Treasury/OECD and Eurostat

Figure 7.16: EU27 unemployment compared to Japan and the USA (% of workforce, ILO measure)

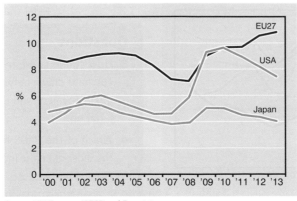

Source: HM Treasury/OECD and Eurostat

Globally, the EU27 average is compared to other major economies in Figure 7.16.

Throughout the early 2000s, unemployment in the USA and Japan experienced unemployment rates of up to half of those experienced in Europe. Note the impact of the recent recession in the USA, and the relatively minor impact of this 'Western' crisis on Japan.

Question

5. Is low unemployment always of benefit to all economic agents in an economy?

Chapter 8

Inflation and Deflation

This chapter looks at the difference between the Retail Price Index and the Consumer Price Index, as well as how they portray trends in price changes over the last decade differently. The chapter goes on to look at recent price changes in various sectors before comparing UK inflation with that of other countries. An examination of the fluctuations in the rate of inflation over the last 10 years follows before a final discussion on the dangers of deflation.

● ● Knowledge and Application: Defining and measuring UK inflation

Inflation is defined as a sustained increase in the general price level.

A key point to note here is that the price of some goods and services might be falling, but the average price of goods and services in the economy is rising. As prices rise, the value of a given amount of money falls as it can purchase fewer goods and services.

There are two main measures of inflation in the UK:

1. Consumer Price Index (CPI)

The CPI index has been used to measure the official rate of inflation in the UK since December 2003 (previously it was the Retail Price Index which is the second measure discussed below). The Bank of England targets inflation at 2.0% according to the CPI measure (see Chapter 9). This measure uses the same methodology as the *Harmonised Index of Consumer Prices* (*HICP*) measure, which is used by economies across the EU. The ECB uses this measure to assess rates of inflation in the Eurozone. The government switched to the CPI measure so that UK inflation could be compared directly with economies in the EU.

The CPI is a weighted index measuring the average price increase of a basket goods and services purchased by a typical household. The Office for National Statistics' (ONS) Expenditure and Food Survey measures the price changes of 700 goods and services purchased from an average household. Each item is weighted according to the proportion of household income that is spent on it. Therefore, if twice as much income is spent by households on clothes than on video games, then clothing should receive twice the weighting.

To ensure that the CPI measure accurately reflects changes in the cost of living, amendments are made annually to the items that are included in the basket so that changes in consumer habits are reflected. In 2012 tablet computers were included for the first time, while processed film was excluded.

Figure 8.1: CPI group weightings 1996 (parts of 1000)

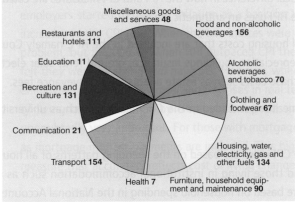

Source: ONS

Figure 8.2: CPI group weightings 2012 (parts of 1000)

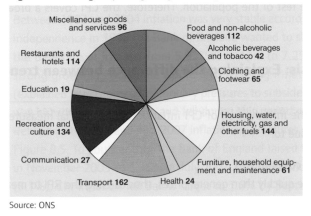

Source: ONS

Figure 8.4: Bank of England base rate 1999-2014

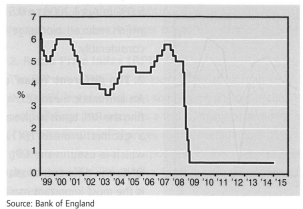

Source: Bank of England

Figure 8.5: CPI in goods and services 1999-2013

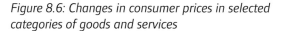
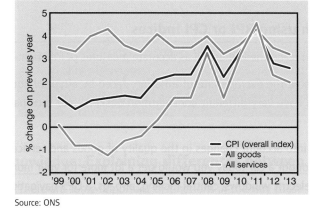

Source: ONS

Figure 8.6: Changes in consumer prices in selected categories of goods and services

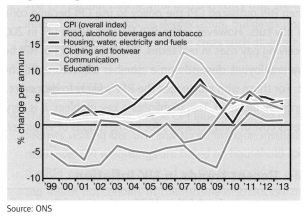

Source: ONS

collapsed, plummeting to 1.1% (CPI) by September 2009. To prevent a sustained period of deflation, the Bank of England slashed the base rate during 2008 and early 2009, reaching just 0.5% by March of that year, where it has remained, despite CPI inflation climbing to 5.2% by September 2011. Inflation then subsided, reaching 2.4% by June 2012, and inflationary pressure remained low, reaching a mere 1.2% in September 2014.

So far we have looked only at overall inflation for goods and services. However, once we disaggregate the data, we can reveal a number of trends which are hidden by aggregate inflation figures:

1. Figure 8.5 shows that for most of the period 1999 to 2013, goods inflation was considerably lower than services inflation. In fact, according to the CPI measure, the average price of goods was falling between 2000 and 2004. Services, by contrast, saw steady price increases of around 3.5-4.5% per annum throughout the period. This means that the cause of low inflation between 1997 and 2004 was due to minimal price rises of goods, while inflation in services was present throughout this period.

2. From 2005 goods inflation started an upward trajectory. Despite falls in goods inflation from 2008 to 2009, goods inflation increased quite dramatically, rising above the rate of services inflation by 2011. Therefore, it was abnormally high inflation in goods, rather than services, which caused overall the monthly rate of CPI inflation to break 5% in the autumns of 2008 and 2011. Since 2011 however, goods inflation has fallen by more than services inflation, bringing down overall inflationary pressure with it.

3. Figure 8.6 shows the very different rates of inflation in different sectors between 1999 and 2013. Price rises in education were high throughout the period due to large private school fee increases and rising university tuition fees. Increases in housing, water, electricity and fuel costs were significantly higher after 2005, as was the case for food price rises. The inflation for clothing and footwear, which had been negative for much of the period, became positive in 2011 underlining the trend of rising goods inflation at that time.

● Application: **International comparison of inflation rates**

Figure 8.7: Average annual percentage change in CPI, 2003-2013

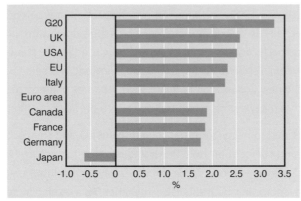

Source: OECD

Figure 8.8: Inflation rates (CPI annual % change) for selected economies 2003-13

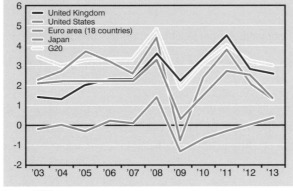

Source: OECD

Figure 8.9: Inflation rates (CPI annual % change) for selected countries 2003-13

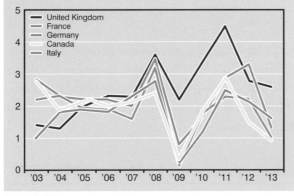

Source: OECD

During the 1970s and much of the 1980s the UK was known as 'the sick man of Europe', in part owing to her poor inflation record. Since the early 1990s the UK's inflation record has been much improved and between the mid-1990s to the mid-2000s the UK's inflation rate compared favourably to that of her competitors. However, from 2005 onwards, the UK inflation rate was generally higher than that of her main competitors, as shown in Figures 8.8 and 8.9. Figure 8.7 shows that between 2003 and 2013 the UK's average inflation rate was above that of most advanced economies, and this continued into 2014 despite UK inflation falling to just 1.2% in September of that year, as the Eurozone economy weakened, and the threat of deflation emerged again in many European economies.

Question

4. Explain why inflation rates in the UK exceeded those of her main competitors between 2006 and 2014.

● Analysis: **Explanations for low UK inflation 1992-2004**

There are several explanations for low inflation in the UK between the early 1990s and the early 2000s. They are:

1. The strong pound

During this period the value of the pound rose significantly, and was at a considerably higher level than during the early 1990s. This put downward pressure on the price of imports, meaning that overall price increases of goods in particular, were restrained. A stronger pound reduced the price of services and finished goods, but also lowered the price of raw materials used to make products in the UK. The UK is a relatively open economy with the value of imports exceeding 30% of GDP. Therefore, lower import prices due to a strong pound had a significant effect.

2. A lack of exogenous shocks

During the 1970s there were a number of hikes in the price of essential sources of energy. The price of oil rose from under $5 per barrel in 1970 to over $25 by 1980. This was a major contributing factor to a period of stagflation (high unemployment and high inflation) in the UK at that time. The period 1992-2004

however, saw no major exogenous shocks, and commodity prices remained reasonably stable which kept cost-push inflationary pressures in check.

3. Competitive product markets

(i) Domestic factors: The 1980s and 1990s saw a period of privatisation and deregulation. This led to greater competition, especially in the utility sector, which put downward pressure on prices. Furthermore, a tougher approach towards competition policy was adopted. The Competition Act of 1998 saw the Competition Commission replacing the Monopolies and Mergers Commission, and the 2002 Enterprise Act gave the new Commission far more power than its predecessor. The effect was to encourage competition across many sectors which put downward pressure on inflation.

(ii) Global factors: During this period many countries joined the WTO and the global economy more generally. The UK faced rising competition from newly-industrialised countries (NICs) such as from China, India and countries in Eastern Europe. These countries have much lower unit labour costs, and thus have a comparative advantage in labour-intensive industries. As a result, UK manufacturers faced stiff competition from overseas and were forced to reduce mark-ups and costs. This effect, along with greater import volumes of goods from NICs, put downward pressure on the price of basic manufactures such as clothing, footwear, and household items, as shown in Figure 8.6.

4. Flexible labour markets

Three factors made the UK's Labour market more flexible during this period:

(i) Greater female participation in the workforce increased the supply of labour and reduced wage-inflationary pressures.

(ii) Significant immigration from outside and inside the EU increased the supply of labour and helped to plug skills shortages in certain industries. On 1st January 2004 ten new countries, mostly from Central and Eastern Europe joined the EU. Afterwards a significant influx of self-selecting, productive workers came to the UK.

(iii) Since the 1980s there has been a significant amount of 'de-unionisation' in the UK, partly due to government policy in the 1980s, and partly due to the relative decline of the more unionised manufacturing sector. Wage bargaining power has declined as a result, reducing cost-push inflationary pressures.

5. Credible monetary policy

After being tasked with controlling inflation in 1998, the Bank of England acted quickly when there were signs of growing inflationary pressure by raising interest rates. Such pre-emptive action and a clearly defined policy framework helped to build faith in the Bank of England's ability to keep inflation within the 1-3% acceptable boundary. This helped to lower *inflationary expectations*, and thus wage demands remained subdued during this period.

● Analysis: **Explanations for the higher rates of inflation 2005-2011**

From 2005-11 inflation has been more volatile than in the previous 15 years, and inflation was undoubtedly higher during this period. There are several reasons for this:

1. Higher commodity prices

From 2007 there has been a significant increase in the price of many commodities, most importantly for the UK economy oil and food have risen in price substantially.

As shown in Figure 8.10 the price of oil rose from $30 per barrel at the start of 2004 to over $130 per barrel in mid-2008. The oil price then collapsed with the onset of the global recession in 2009 but recovered

Figure 8.10: Brent crude oil price, Jan 2000-Oct 2014

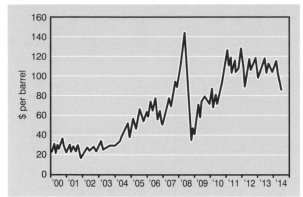

Source: US Department for Energy

strongly. In 2012 the global oil price remained high despite faltering recoveries in most developed economies. The historically high average oil price between 2005 and 2011 was due to growing demand from developing economies, and slow production growth due to dwindling stocks. Higher oil prices push up the cost of production of many goods and services, thus contributing to higher cost-push inflationary pressures.

Figure 8.11: UK consumer food prices index (2010 = 100)

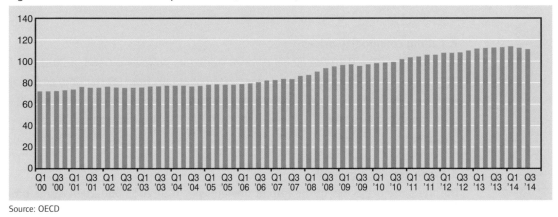

Source: OECD

Figure 8.11 shows that food prices started to rise rapidly after 2006, owing to more wheat being used for bio-fuels rather than food production, increased global demand due to world population growth, and rising demand for meat by consumers in NICs. Although food prices fell back during the global recession of 2008-09 they have since risen, and by the start of 2014 UK consumer food prices were 14% higher than in 2010.

2. A weaker pound

After the peak in the trade-weighted value of sterling in early 2007 the pound depreciated considerably, losing almost 30% of its value by early 2009, as shown in Figure 5.14. Despite gains against the Euro since then, the pound remains considerably weaker than during the NICE decade. This caused the price of imports to rise, raising the overall price level.

3. Inflation and wage inflation in NICs

Since the mid-2000s a number of NICs, including India and China, have been suffering from high inflation, and high wage inflation. In China for example, the wage gap to advanced economies has shrunk rapidly in recent years, in part due to hikes in the minimum wage. This has caused the price of cheap manufactured imports to rise, and overall goods inflation increased as a result, as shown in Figure 8.5.

4. VAT increases

The rate of Value Added Tax (VAT), which is paid on most goods and services in the UK was cut from 17.5% to 15% on 1st December 2008 to try to stimulate consumption as the economy fell into a deep recession. The rate of VAT returned to 17.5% in January 2010, and was then raised to 20% on 4th January 2011 by the new Chancellor George Osborne, as part of the government's fiscal deficit reduction strategy. Both of these VAT increases had a significant impact in pushing up the price of goods and services.

● Analysis: **Explanations for falling inflation 2012-2014**

Figure 8.12: UK monthly CPI inflation rates, Jan 2011-Sept 2014

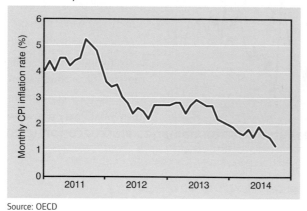

Source: OECD

Since the monthly rate of CPI inflation peaked in September 2011 at 5.2% there has been a strong downward trend in the rate of inflation, to just 1.2% in September 2014. There are several reasons for this:

1. A stronger Pound

As shown in Figure 5.14 the pound rose in value consistently throughout 2013 and 2014, putting downward pressure on the price of imported goods and services.

2. Falling commodity prices

As shown in Figure 8.10 the global oil price started its downward trend in 2012 and fell considerably in 2014 to less than $85 per barrel due to increased oil supply from US fracking, and weakening demand for oil due to a slowdown in growth in major emerging markets and the Eurozone. Figure 8.11 shows that food price growth slowed from 2012 and actually fell in 2014. Falling commodity prices reduced cost-push pressures significantly.

3. Weak earnings growth

Despite large decreases in the rate of unemployment in 2013 and 2014, wage growth has remained extremely low, and was just 0.8% in September 2014 despite a record fall in unemployment. This has helped to reduce both demand-pull and cost-push pressures.

Extension material: 'Core' inflation

A measure of 'core' inflation can be useful as it excludes price changes in volatile items such as food and energy. Therefore, it is a reasonable measure of 'underlying' inflationary pressure in the economy. However, as high commodity prices could be a more frequent feature than during the NICE decade, cost-push, rather than demand-pull pressures might well be the main cause of inflation for several years to come. 'Core' inflation therefore, might not be a very good predictor of actual changes in the rate of inflation.

● Knowledge: **Deflation**

Deflation is a sustained **fall** in the general price level. It is important to distinguish between deflation which may be harmful, and deflation that does not harm macroeconomic performance.

(i) Deflation may occur due to technological advances and productivity gains that cause

Oil prices fell considerably during 2014.

long-run economic growth. As the long-run aggregate supply curve shifts to the right, there is downward pressure on the price level. This is known as *benign* deflation.

(ii) However, a lack of aggregate demand may also cause the overall price level to fall. This has been a persistent problem in Japan since the 1990s, as shown in Figures 8.7 and 8.8. This type is known as *malign* deflation. Since the global recession of 2008-09 the European Central Bank and other policy makers have feared that the Eurozone may be headed for a period of Japanese-style deflation, and have taken unprecedented steps to try to avoid it. This danger loomed large in September 2014, with Eurozone inflation falling to just 0.3%.

● Analysis: **Reasons why malign deflation damages macroeconomic performance**

There are several reasons why deflation due to a lack of aggregate demand is a problem:

1. Deferred consumption
If consumers see prices falling today, they will postpone consumption as prices will be lower in the future. Therefore, consumption and aggregate demand will fall, reducing growth and employment. The resulting fall in the price level further entrenches the deflation problem.

2. Rising real value of debt
As prices fall, nominal wages may fall as well. Employers may try to justify cuts in nominal wages when prices are falling. In addition, as aggregate demand in the economy is weak, workers are in a weak bargaining position. As nominal wages fall, it becomes harder for households to repay their debts, as their nominal value remains unchanged. This means that households must allocate a greater proportion of income towards debt repayment, and cut back on consumption.

3. Monetary policy becomes ineffective
Deflation can cause monetary policy to become a significantly less powerful policy instrument. To try to boost aggregate demand and prevent a persistent period of deflation from occurring, a central bank will cut interest rates. However, if interest rates are cut by 1%, but prices fall by 2%, the **real interest rate** has actually risen, which encourages saving and discourages consumer spending. Moreover, once interest rates have been cut to zero, there is nothing more that interest changes can do to inflate aggregate demand, thus rendering interest rate cuts ineffective, and central banks will have to resort to printing money (quantitative easing), as is the policy in Japan and the Eurozone today.

4. Large fiscal deficits and debt burdens emerge
As monetary policy becomes ineffective in stimulating aggregate demand, the government must adopt an expansionary fiscal policy instead. A sustained budget deficit could lead to excessive levels of national debt being accumulated, which will create a drag on growth in the long term. This is what happened in Japan, where national debt reached 227% of GDP by 2014.

Essay Questions

5. Examine the effects of a rise in the price of oil upon UK macroeconomic performance.

6. Evaluate the view that adjusting interest rates is the best way to manage the rate of inflation in the UK.

7. 'Deflation is always bad for macroeconomic performance'. To what extent do you agree with this statement?

Chapter 9

Monetary Policy in the UK

Monetary policy is defined as government policy regarding interest rates, exchange rates and the money supply. Since 1992 the UK has had a floating exchange rate, and thus the value of the pound is not deliberately altered by policy makers. Until recently monetary policy in effect meant the setting of interest rates, but in 2009 the Bank of England started to use a new policy, **quantitative easing**. The Monetary Policy Committee at the Bank of England is the focal point of this chapter; the committee members themselves, the tools they use to target inflation, and how successful they have been in achieving their objective.

● ● Knowledge and Application: The UK monetary policy framework

On 6th May 1997 the newly-elected government announced plans to give the Bank of England independence, which was achieved under the 1998 Bank of England Act. The Monetary Policy Committee (MPC) at the Bank of England was given operational independence for setting interest rates to achieve **price stability**, while supporting the government's targets for growth and employment. Those in favour of independence argued that by being free of political interference, the Bank of England should gain credibility for controlling inflation. The MPC contains 9 members.

The MPC's task is to achieve the inflation target by adjusting the base rate. The base rate (also known as the repo rate) is the interest rate at which the Bank of England lends to commercial banks. Since 2003 the Bank of England has had an inflation target of 2.0% on the CPI measure, with a symmetrical 'acceptable boundary' of between 1 and 3%.

Figure 9.1: Bank of England base rate (%) 1999-2014

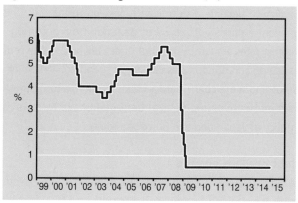

Source: Bank of England

It takes up to two years for the full effect of a change in the interest rate to have its impact upon aggregate demand and therefore inflation. As a result, the MPC makes interest rate decisions to try to achieve the inflation target in two years time, and therefore acts in a *pre-emptive* manner, rather than in response to recent changes in the inflation rate. The MPC gathers information to predict inflation into the future, and adjust the base rate to try to bring future inflation back to target. One good example of the pre-emptive setting of the interest rate came in late 2008. The Bank of England cut the base rate from 4.5% to 0.5% between October 2008 and March 2009 despite the fact that inflation remained above target throughout this period. In fact, when the base rate was cut on 4th October 2008 the previous month's CPI inflation rate was 5.2%, the highest level since 1992. The MPC was cutting rates as they predicted a fall in core inflationary pressure as the economy fell into recession.

The MPC meets for two and a half days each month. They usually meet on the first Wednesday and Thursday of each month with a half day 'pre-meeting' on the Friday before. On the Wednesday members hear a wealth of data on the domestic and global economy from Bank of England economists and regional representatives. The data includes developments in trade, investment, financial markets, productivity, the budget balance and many other indicators. Ultimately the Bank is trying to decide how strong domestic demand will be relative to the productive capacity of the economy, in effect, predicting the future output gap. If domestic demand is growing faster than the economy's productive potential then inflationary pressure will be forecast to grow, and interest rates should be raised.

On the basis of the data the MPC members must decide if inflation is set to hit the target in two years time. Members then vote on whether to hold, raise, or cut the base rate. Each member has one vote, and the majority decision is implemented.

There were disagreements between MPC members over base rate changes in August and September 2014 for the first time since July 2011. In spite of very weak wage growth through 2013 and 2014, Ian McCafferty and Martin Weale expected a sharp rise in wage inflation as unemployment fell below 6% and the UK economy would start to run up against capacity constraints. The pair voted in favour of a 0.25% rise in the base rate but the other seven members of the MPC including Mark Carney, the Governor of the Bank of England, voted in favour of holding the base rate at 0.5% citing a benign inflationary outlook. Since the end of the recession in 2009 there has been ongoing speculation as to when interest rates will start going up. Mark Carney has promised that when base rare rises do come, they will be "gradual and limited".

Questions

1. The Monetary Policy Committee (MPC) is most likely to raise interest rates if:
   A. Unemployment is rising.
   B. The exchange rate is appreciating.
   C. The growth of the money supply is decreasing.
   D. Domestic demand is set to rise above the level of potential GDP.

2. Explain the difficulty in measuring the size of an output gap.

Due to the important role of expectations, monetary policy is most likely to be successful if the Bank of England has *credibility*. That is, the public believe in the MPC's ability to control inflation. A number of measures have been used to try to achieve this:

(i) The workings of the MPC are **transparent**, and members are accountable. The minutes of the meeting are published two weeks after the meeting, and show how each member voted. Those in the minority are asked to state the action they would have preferred.

(ii) Members of the MPC regularly appear before parliamentary committees, usually the **Treasury Select Committee**, to answer questions about their decisions. The MPC is also accountable to the **Court of the Bank**, comprising experts in commerce, industry and finance.

(iii) If the rate of inflation goes outside of the 1-3% 'acceptable' limits the Governor of the Bank of England must write an **open letter** to the Chancellor of the Exchequer to explain why the inflation target has been missed, and how he/she intends to rectify this.

(iv) The **Inflation Report**, published each quarter, provides details on recent developments in the economy and monetary policy, justifying the MPC's actions.

(v) Perhaps most importantly, the MPC is made up of **experts from a wide variety of backgrounds** including academics, monetary policy experts and economists from industry.

The 9 members of the Monetary Policy Committee (October 2014)

Mark Carney	Governor of the Bank of England
Ben Broadbent	Deputy Governor (responsible for Monetary Policy)
Sir Jon Cunliffe	Deputy Governor (responsible for Financial Stability)
Nemat Shafik	Deputy Governor (responsible for Markets and Banking)
Andy Haldane	Executive Director, Monetary Analysis & Chief Economist
Kristin Forbes	External member, Professor of Management and Global Economics at MIT
David Miles	External member, former Chief UK Economist of Morgan Stanley
Ian McCafferty	External member, former Chief Economic Adviser to the CBI
Martin Weale	External member, former Director of NIESR

● Analysis: **Why does the UK have an inflation target?**

There are several advantages from having a specific 2.0% inflation target:

1. Reducing inflationary expectations

By having a *credible* 2.0% target, workers will moderate their wage claims accordingly, as they can achieve real income growth without large pay demands. This reduces cost-push inflationary pressures. Similarly, businesses will avoid large price increases if prices across the economy are not expected to rise significantly.

2. Failure of targeting 'intermediate variables'

Intermediate variables (i.e. variables which influence the rate of inflation such as the exchange rate or the money supply) can be targeted rather than inflation itself. During the 1980s there was no specific inflation target. Instead, the Thatcher government tried, unsuccessfully, to control the money supply, which continued to grow. Targeting inflation directly allows policy-makers to consider all the factors that influence inflation, rather than fixating on one or two.

3. Keeping fiat money credible

The value of money is no longer tied to gold. Instead, *fiat* money is only worth something because people believe it has value, and one of the most important jobs of any government is to preserve the value of money. Therefore, it is beneficial to have a monetary policy framework which protects against inflation and helps people to believe that their money will have almost the same worth tomorrow as today.

4. Success of inflation targeting elsewhere

Inflation targeting has proved effective in other countries, particularly in New Zealand and Canada after they adopted the policy in the early 1990s.

● Analysis: **The transmission mechanism of monetary policy**

Changes in interest rates affect inflation primarily through their impact on aggregate demand, and also through changes in the price of imported goods and services. A fall in interest rates, such as the fall in the base rate from 5.0% to 0.5% between April 2008 and March 2009 could impact upon the economy via a number of channels:

1. Household saving and borrowing

Lower interest rates reduce the cost of borrowing, and reduce the return on saving. This should raise the level of borrowing and reduce the savings ratio, thus increasing consumption and aggregate demand. Demand for consumer durables (e.g. cars, computers) should rise significantly, as they are usually purchased on credit.

2. Mortgage repayments and effective disposable income

According to the Financial Services Authority (FSA) around 70% of mortgages in the UK are variable rate mortgages. Therefore, a fall in the interest rate will mean that monthly mortgage repayments will fall, increasing the effective disposable income of homeowners. This should boost consumption and hence aggregate demand. This effect is especially significant for the UK, as around 67% of households were 'owner-occupied' in 2012, far higher than most of Europe.

3. Asset prices and the 'wealth effect'

As interest rates fall, the return on holding cash savings accounts diminishes. Therefore savers and investors in search of a better return are more likely to purchase equities or property, thus increasing their demand and value. Furthermore, more people will be tempted to buy property when interest rates are low, as mortgage payments will be lower. This puts further upward pressure on property prices. As asset prices rise, people see their wealth value increase and 'feel' richer, boosting consumer confidence and consumption. In addition, some households will take out loans against the rising value of their properties, adding to consumption. This is known as **equity withdrawal**.

4. Investment and the 'hurdle rate'

At any point in time firms have a number of potential investment projects. The hurdle rate is the minimum expected return a company demands before it goes ahead with a project given the risks involved. Many investments are funded through borrowing. As interest rates fall, the expected return of a project rises as the cost of the project has fallen. Therefore more projects become profitable, so more will go ahead, thus increasing overall investment and aggregate demand.

5. The exchange rate, net exports and import prices

As interest rates fall, there is a 'hot money' outflow as international investors see a fall on their return from keeping money in UK banks. This causes demand for the pound to fall, resulting in currency depreciation. As a result exports become more attractive while imports become more expensive, resulting in a rise in net exports, aggregate demand, and inflation. Furthermore, a rise in the price in imports directly raises the price level.

Figure 9.2: The monetary policy transmission mechanism

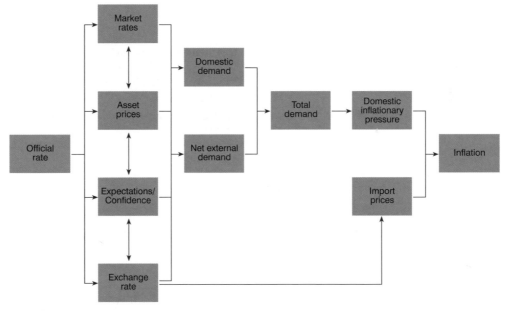

Source: Bank of England

● Evaluation: The effects of a fall in interest rates

Making accurate forecasts over the impact of a fall in interest rates is difficult for several reasons:

1. **Time lags** – Commercial banks do not immediately adjust their retail interest rates in response to a fall in the base rate, and it takes a further year for the full impact of a change in aggregate demand to affect inflation.

2. **Asymmetric impact on households** – Individuals who rely heavily on savings (e.g. pensioners) will see their income from interest fall in response to a fall in the base rate, and thus their spending may fall. However, this effect is outweighed by higher borrowing, less saving and more spending from most households, increasing aggregate demand overall.

3. **Asymmetric impact on firms** – When interest rates fall some firms will see their income from cash deposits fall, potentially reducing their level of investment. However, across all firms, lower interest rates tend to boost investment levels due to the lower cost of borrowing to finance investment projects.

4. **Some mortgages are fixed rate** – some mortgages in the UK offer fixed rates of interest, and thus monthly repayments will not fall in response to a base rate cut until the term of the fixed rate expires, and the terms of the mortgage are renegotiated. However, most mortgages in the UK are 'variable rate'.

Figure 9.3: Bank Rate and quoted interest rates on new household borrowing

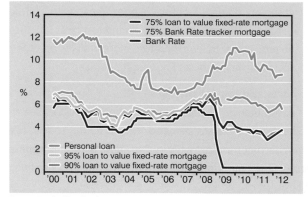

Source: Bank of England

5. **De-coupling** – When the Bank of England cut the base rate dramatically between late 2008 and early 2009, rates on key personal loans such as credit cards and overdrafts actually increased as shown in Figure 9.3. This was due to banks trying to repair their balance sheets in the wake of the financial crisis, higher interbank lending rates and the banks attaching a higher 'risk premium' to lending during a time of recession and enormous uncertainty.

6. **Willingness to borrow/lend** – Despite the significant base rate cuts between late 2008 and early 2009, the savings rate rose considerably due to falling consumer confidence, and households became less willing to borrow as consumers prepared for a 'rainy day'. Simultaneously, banks became less willing to lend, which harmed SMEs who struggled to access much needed credit.

● Evaluation: How well has the UK monetary policy framework worked?

Since the Bank of England was granted control of the base rate of interest with the objective of controlling inflation in 1997, most would argue that the effect has been broadly positive, especially in the first 10 years. There are several reasons for this:

Figure 9.4: UK CPI and Bank of England Base Rate, 1999-2014

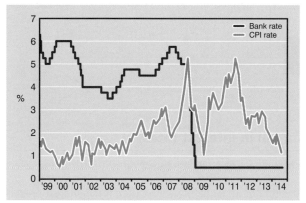

Source:ONS, Bank of England

● From Bank of England independence in May 1997 right through to March 2007 monthly CPI inflation was within the target range the vast majority of the time.

● The MPC were praised by the House of Commons Treasury Select Committee for establishing a credible inflation targeting record.

● The UK's inflation performance was stronger than most of her European and North American competitors between 1997 and 2007.

● The Bank of England was effective in pre-empting future inflationary pressure and taking action as demonstrated by repeated rate rises in early 2004, when the MPC lifted the bank rate by a full percentage point which caused inflation to fall back to target by the end of 2005.

● In 1997 Bank of England Governor Mervyn King acknowledged the Bank of England's role in supporting other macroeconomic objectives, particularly growth and employment. He stated that central bankers should not be 'inflation nutters' i.e. they should not focus purely on controlling inflation at the expense of growth and employment, a popular criticism of the European Central Bank (ECB). The MPC's significant base rate cuts in 2001 were effective in preventing a major downturn.

However, there has also been some criticism of the MPC, which has grown since 2007:

● The UK's inflation performance worsened considerably after the beginning of the financial crisis in the autumn of 2007, both relative to the UK's main competitors and in relation to the inflation target.

Between September 2007 and September 2012 CPI inflation was above the 3% upper acceptable boundary for 40 out of 60 months. During this time Mervyn King had to write 14 open letters to the Chancellor explaining why the MPC failed to keep inflation within the 1-3% boundary, whereas no letters were written during the previous 10 years.

● Some argue that the MPC have not always reacted quickly enough to changes in inflationary pressure. Inflationary pressure started to rise from the beginning of 2006 but the MPC did not raise the base rate until August of that year. More significant however, was the MPC's late reaction in cutting interest rates as the UK economy fell into a deep recession in 2008. GDP had been falling since the second quarter of 2008, but inflation reached 5.2% in September of that year largely due to a temporary commodity price spike. Critics argue that the MPC should have recognised that these pressures were temporary, and that underlying inflationary pressure at the time was falling dramatically due to collapsing demand and rising unemployment. The Bank of England cut the base rate aggressively from 5.0% in October 2008 to 0.5% in March 2009, but this was not enough to stop CPI inflation falling well below target, and the RPI measure indicating a significant period of deflation for much of 2009.

● Some believe that the MPC's objectives have become blurred in recent years, thus eroding their credibility for inflation targeting. Critics argue that since the 2008-09 recession more emphasis has been put on growth rather than targeting inflation. During 2010 inflationary pressure grew significantly, and CPI inflation averaged 4.5% in 2011. Yet the Bank of England did not raise interest rates, keeping the base rate at the historic low of 0.5%. The fact that the UK economy narrowly avoided falling back into recession in 2011 and 2012 suggests that the Bank of England sided with supporting growth rather than controlling inflation. Supporters of the MPC are quick to point out that much of this inflation was due to temporary factors beyond their control (such as the VAT rise to 20% and energy price increases) and that underlying pressures remained weak. Inflation did fall back to below 3% by May 2012 and continued to fall through 2013 to reach just 1.2% in September 2014, which supports the view that interest rates should have remained at their historical low. To bring some clarity to the Bank of England's position on supporting growth and employment Mark Carney, the new Governor of the Bank of England from July 2013 announced some explicit 'forward guidance' on the conduct of future monetary policy (see below) just one month after taking up his position.

● Critics have argued that monetary policy has been operating under a 'one tool, one target' framework which has focussed too much on targeting overall price increases while ignoring the impact of policy instruments on key asset prices such as house prices. Although monetary policy was effective in controlling overall price increases during the NICE decade (1997-2007), double digit house price inflation was the norm. In the UK and the US an extended period of low interest rates and high credit availability, especially in the early 2000s, fuelled a house price bubble which may have boosted consumer confidence and prevented deflation in the short term, but increased the risk of deflation when the housing bubble burst in 2007-08. In the wake of the financial crisis of 2008 there has been a consensus amongst economists that central banks should do more to prevent excessive lending and asset bubbles emerging in order to reduce the risk they pose to financial stability. The Financial Services Act 2012, which came into force in April 2013, was a direct response to this. It established an independent Financial Policy Committee (FPC), a new prudential regulator as a subsidiary of the Bank, and created new responsibilities for the supervision of financial market infrastructure. The (FPC) contributes to the achievement of the Bank's financial stability objective. It is charged with taking action to remove or reduce systemic risks with a view to protecting and enhancing the resilience of the UK financial system.

Recent changes to the policy framework: Forward guidance

Through 2010 and 2011 inflation was above the 'acceptable' upper boundary of 3% every month but the Bank kept the base rate at 0.5%. This was partly due to the fact that the inflationary pressure was largely due to 'cost-push' factors such as rising global food, energy and other commodity prices which are beyond

the control of the MPC, but it became clear that the Bank of England was clearly intent on supporting growth and employment during the faltering recovery. Critics said that the Bank's objectives had become blurred, and ill-defined. To deal with this the MPC voted to provide some explicit 'forward guidance' on the future conduct of monetary policy at its meeting on 1st August 2013. The MPC said it intended to maintain an expansive monetary policy, continuing with a record low base rate and assets purchases (quantitative easing, see below) until 'economic slack' had been substantially reduced, provided this did not entail material risks to either price stability or financial stability. In particular, the MPC said it intended not to raise the Bank Rate from 0.5% at least until the unemployment rate fell to a threshold of 7%, subject to the conditions below. The guidance linking Bank Rate and asset sales to the unemployment threshold would cease to hold if any of the following three 'knockouts' were breached:

1. In the MPC's view, it became more likely than not, that CPI inflation 18 to 24 months ahead would be 0.5 percentage points or more above the 2% target.

2. Medium-term inflation expectations no longer remained sufficiently well anchored.

3. The Financial Policy Committee (FPC) judged that the stance of monetary policy posed a significant threat to financial stability (e.g. the emergence of asset bubbles) that could not be contained by the range of policy actions available to the FPC, the Financial Conduct Authority and the Prudential Regulation Authority.

The unemployment rate fell below 7% in February 2014 yet the Bank of England did not raise the base rate due to falling inflationary pressure and a benign inflationary outlook.

Quantitative easing

By March 2009 the base rate had been cut to a historic low of 0.5% in an attempt to boost aggregate demand, but the UK economy remained in a deep recession and there was a continued threat of deflation. As a result, the MPC decided to try something new; **Quantitative Easing (QE)**.

By late 2012 £375bn had been created electronically by the Bank of England and placed into an 'Asset Purchase Facility'. This money is then used to buy illiquid assets, mostly government bonds, from financial institutions in exchange for more liquid cash. As a result, financial institutions have more loanable funds which can be passed onto households and firms, thus boosting aggregate demand, and putting upward pressure on prices. As the Bank of England is a big buyer in the bonds ('gilts') market, higher demand for bonds increases their price, reducing the yields and effective interest rates on bonds, which are the benchmark for some mortgage rates, bank overdraft rates and business borrowing rates. This should encourage borrowing and spending. Crucially, the Bank of England uses the newly-created money to purchase gilts from private investors such as pension funds and insurance companies. These investors typically do not want to hold on to this money, because it yields a low return. So they tend to use it to purchase other assets, such as corporate bonds and shares. That lowers longer-term borrowing costs and encourages the issuance of new equities and bonds, as well as increasing asset prices, confidence and overall spending in the economy.

Arguments in favour of quantitative easing

1. The supply of credit should increase due to greater liquidity in the financial system, as should the demand for credit due to lower interest rates. This should boost aggregate demand and put upward pressure on prices, thus reducing deflationary risks.

2. The Bank of England base rate cannot be lowered much further, thus new policy instruments are needed.

3. The policy could stimulate lending more directly than a base rate cut due to its direct impact on several benchmark lending rates.

4. The policy may have prevented recession and a descent into a deflationary spiral in Japan between 2001 and 2006.

The Bank of England introduced quantitative easing in March 2009 and has now purchased £375bn worth of mainly government bonds to boost liquidity in the economy.

Arguments against quantitative easing

1. A significant rise in the money supply always poses the risk of causing inflation.

2. Critics have argued that elements of the QE policy are a sign that the Bank of England has become blurred in their objectives. Many argue that an unstated goal of QE is to help the ailing financial system to recover from the financial crisis by injecting much needed liquidity, which should prevent financial institutions from collapsing and guard against risks posed from potential default by Eurozone governments. In addition, many claim another unstated goal of QE is to help the UK government borrow at reduced rates of interest, which is particularly important given the large size of the budget deficit since the 2008-09 recession. Finally, some argue that elements of the QE policy show that the Bank of England has become more focussed on boosting growth rather than controlling inflation. For example, the MPC announced the creation of a further £75bn to be injected into the economy in October 2011, at a time when inflation was well above target at 5.0%.

3. Since the asset purchase programme was extended beyond the initial £200bn in October 2010, the amount of liquid money on bank's balance sheets has risen by around 58% but loans issued to households and businesses have remained almost unchanged. This suggests that banks are holding onto this extra liquidity to improve their balance sheets, rather than increasing their lending, as the policy aimed to do. The fear is that when macroeconomic conditions improve and confidence returns, banks could increase lending significantly, thus increasing the effective money supply and inflation. However, the Bank of England could reverse the QE process and sell bonds back to the market if it looks like inflation may go above target.

4. There is strong evidence that QE has added substantially to wealth inequality. The policy deliberately aims to increase asset prices. Wealthier households own more assets such as houses and shares, and thus they gain far more from pumped up asset prices than less wealthy households. On the other hand households with large investments have seen very low returns on these investments as a result of QE. Those in work approaching retirement found a marked fall in annuity rates after 2010.

5. Towards the end of 2012 Mervyn King acknowledged that QE might be reaching the limit of its effectiveness. On 1st August 2012 the Treasury and the Bank of England launched the **Funding for Lending** bank scheme, where commercial banks can borrow from the Bank of England at low rates of

interest (just 0.75%) on the condition that they increase lending to households and small businesses, with penalties if this was not achieved. In its early stages, the scheme was broadly deemed to be a success.

Extension material: The relationship between money supply (M4) and inflation

M4 is a measure of the broad money supply in the economy and is often driven by bank lending. The general relationship between the money supply and the price level is a proportional one, as stated by the famous monetarist Milton Friedman when he stated that 'inflation is always and everywhere a monetary phenomenon'. The Fisher equation supports this view: MV = PT where M = money supply, V = velocity of circulation, P = price level and T = number of transactions or real output. If V and T remain constant, which is not unrealistic in the short run, a rise in the money supply should directly lead to a rise in the price level. However, V has varied considerably in recent years. Since 2008-09, low consumer and business confidence due to macroeconomic uncertainty caused agents to hold onto their money for longer as they are less willing to spend.

Figure 9.5: M4 broad money and Nominal GDP

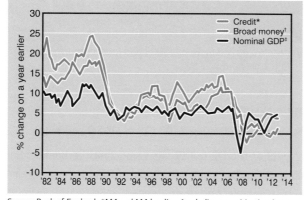

Source: Bank of England; *M4 and M4 lending (excluding securitisations) growth prior to 1998 Q4, and equivalent measures excluding the deposits of, and borrowing by, intermediate OFCs thereafter; †M4 excluding intermediate other financial corporations (OFCs); ‡At current market prices (real GDP).

If broad money growth exceeds nominal GDP growth (the rise in the value of output of goods and services) you would expect significant inflation to be the result, as there would be more money chasing goods and services, thus 'bidding up' their prices. However, as shown in Figure 9.5 broad money growth was considerably higher than nominal GDP growth for much of 2000-2008, without causing significant inflation. There are a few possible explanations for this: money, especially consumer credit, was being used to purchase large quantities of foreign goods; large quantities of money were being used to buy assets which raised asset price (e.g. housing price) inflation but not wider inflation; broad money growth during this period was concentrated in the hands of OFCs (Other Financial Corporations) such as pension and private equity funds, who do not spend lots of money in the conventional sense; and lastly money may have been borrowed in the UK, adding to the money supply figures but spent of assets abroad.

There was a rapid fall in broad money growth from 2008 onwards, largely due to the Credit Crunch, where banks reduced lending considerably. The rapid fall in money supply growth in 2008-09 was a major cause of inflation falling below target by June 2009, and the threat of deflation became very real. This was a major justification for Quantitative Easing, which aimed to boost the money supply and reduce the risk of deflation. The £125bn of asset purchases made by the Bank of England in the nine months to June 2012 were a major factor in bringing about a rise in money supply growth in 2012. However, nominal GDP only rose by £30bn, providing more evidence that commercial banks were not passing on the money received from their sale of bonds to the Bank of England. This highlights the fact that the relationship between the money supply and inflation is far from straightforward.

Questions

3. Explain how quantitative easing can be used to prevent deflation.

4. 'The Bank of England has been very successful in controlling inflation since being given independence in 1997'. To what extent do you agree with this statement?

Chapter 10

UK Fiscal Policy

In this chapter we explore recent changes to tax rates and trends in government expenditure under both the Labour and Coalition governments.

● Knowledge: **Defining fiscal policy**

Fiscal policy is government policy regarding taxation, government spending and borrowing. It is primarily a demand-management policy used to influence macroeconomic variables such as aggregate demand, but it can also be used to influence the supply side of the economy, and it also has a large microeconomic impact as it addresses market failures.

There are several objectives of fiscal policy:

1. To manage demand in the economy.

2. To fund government spending.

3. To correct market failures, such as the problem of public goods and externalities.

4. To redistribute income and wealth.

5. To improve the supply side performance of the economy.

● Knowledge: **Types of taxation**

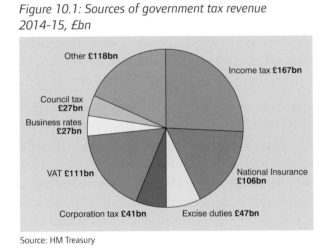

Figure 10.1: Sources of government tax revenue 2014-15, £bn

Source: HM Treasury

Total tax revenue for the 2014-15 financial year is expected to be £648bn. Business rates and Council Tax are collected by local authorities, but the majority of taxes are collected by HM Revenue and Customs.

Direct taxes are taxes levied directly on an individual or organisation, such as income tax, corporation tax or national insurance contributions (NICs). As shown by Figure 10.1, income tax is the most important contributor to government revenue, followed by VAT and NICs. Direct taxes tend to be **progressive**, where a higher proportion of income is paid in tax as the income level increases.

Indirect taxes are taxes levied on goods and services, effectively taxing expenditure. Figure 10.1 shows that Value Added Tax (VAT) is the most important source of indirect tax revenue. Other indirect taxes include excise duties, air passenger duty, customs duties and landfill tax. Unlike direct taxes, the burden of the tax can be passed onto a third party. VAT, for example, is levied on the producer, but they can choose to pass some of the burden of the tax onto the consumer. Indirect taxes tend to be **regressive**, where a higher proportion of income is paid in tax as the income level falls.

Application: **Changes in UK tax rates**

Table 10.1: Changes in UK income tax and VAT rates

| Year | Income tax rates (%) | | | | VAT rate (%) |
	Starting rate	Basic	Higher	New Top Rate	Standard rate
1978					8
1979	-	33	83	-	15
1988	-	25	40	-	
1991					17.5
1992	25	25	40	-	
1997	20	24	40	-	
1999	10	22	40	-	
2008	-	20	40	-	15
2010	-	20	40	50	17.5
2011					20
2013	-	20	40	45	20

Table 10.1 shows a shift in the burden of taxation away from direct taxes such as income tax, towards higher indirect taxes such as VAT. Much of this shift occurred under the Conservative Government 1979-97. Such a shift is controversial, as it made the tax system less progressive overall. This is partly responsible for the significant rise in rise in the level of income inequality under the Conservatives, as explained in Chapter 4.

Analysis: **Income tax and tax credits**

The reason for the cuts in income tax shown in Table 10.1 was to increase the incentive to work. Cuts in direct taxation encourage more people to join the labour force or work longer hours, thus boosting labour supply and supply-side growth.

A major initiative of the Labour government (1997-2010) was to vastly extend **tax credits** to poor working families, beginning with the Working Families Tax Credit in 1999. This was then split into two separate tax credits in 2003: the Working Tax Credit is an additional benefit to working individuals or families on low incomes. The Child Tax Credit is paid directly to the main carer of the family, and is designed to tackle child poverty. It is paid regardless of whether people work and families on any income can receive the Child Tax Credit, although high earning households became ineligible from April 2013. The actual amount of child tax credits that a person may receive depends on these factors: the level of their income, the number of children they have, whether the children are receiving Disability Living Allowance and the education status of any children over 16.

Like cuts in income tax during the 1980s, the main aim of tax credits is to **make work pay**. This should reduce the unemployment trap, as the incentive to work is greater. Many earners on low income face very high effective marginal tax rates, as earning more, perhaps through working longer hours will result in the withdrawal of certain benefits (e.g. housing benefit or free school meals) often combined with paying the 20% tax rate on the additional income earned. The Working Tax Credit, therefore, aims to boost the effective take-home income from work for low earners.

The abolition of the 10% starting rate of income tax in 2008 was widely criticised as many households on low income, and young childless single workers in particular, would see their disposable income reduced significantly, reducing the incentive to work. In the face of heavy criticism, the Labour Government expanded their tax credits program to offset this. The Coalition adopted a key Liberal Democrat election pledge to raise the tax free allowance to £10,000 by the end of Parliament in 2015, thereby increasing the incentive to work and lifting millions out of income tax altogether. The tax free allowance had been raised from £6,475 in 2010-11 to £10,000 2014-15.

The Chancellor Alastair Darling announced in the 2009 budget a new top rate of tax at 50% of income above £150,000 which came into effect in April 2010. The Treasury believed it would raise an extra £2.5bn per year. The arguments in favour of the new tax rate include:

- It would help to reduce the size of the large budget deficit.

- It could help to redistribute income.

- The revenue could be used to invest in public services.

- A populist view coming out of the financial crisis and Great Recession was that high earners created the economic problems but were not suffering to the same extent as those on low incomes or those made unemployed, and thus the new top rate was fair, showing that 'we're all in it together'.

Arguments against include:

- Individuals affected may reduce their spending due to a decline in disposable income, with adverse effects on employment and other tax revenues such as VAT.

- It creates a disincentive, reducing income earned and tax taken.

- International labour mobility has increased significantly over the last 20 years, particularly for high earners. Therefore, a 'brain drain' may occur as productive workers migrate to lower tax regimes.

- It may reduce inward foreign direct investment (FDI), and cause companies to move overseas, particularly in financial services where high pay is common.

- It may lead to significant tax avoidance through converting income into capital gains which is taxed at a much lower rate, or moving income to offshore tax havens, or bringing income forward (as was the case in 2009-10 before the rate came into effect).

A Treasury report published in March 2012 revealed that the 50% tax rate was probably yielding only £1bn per year or less, or even a negative yield. In the 2012 budget the Chancellor George Osborne announced a cut in the new top rate to 45%, effective from April 2013.

Evaluation material: Income and substitution effects

If income taxes are cut this will increase the disposable income earned from every hour of work, which may entice the individual to work longer hours. This is known as the **substitution effect**, where the individual substitutes leisure time for work. The **income effect** works the other way. A worker might have a target level of post-tax annual income they wish to obtain, which can now be achieved by working fewer hours. Thus, the individual chooses to work less in favour of more leisure time.

Evidence suggests that which effect is greater depends on the individual, but some patterns within groups can be identified. Hours worked by females tend to be quite responsive to income tax cuts, while hours worked by males are almost entirely unresponsive. Both male and female participation rates are very responsive. Overall, direct tax cuts do increase the incentive to work.

● Analysis: **Corporation tax**

Both the Labour and Coalition governments have followed policies of significantly reducing the corporation tax rate. There are several reasons why such a policy has been pursued. The exchequer has been keen to boost investment which is usually funded from post-tax profits, while continuing to attract large sums of inward FDI from overseas in a world where capital is highly mobile. Furthermore, lower corporation tax rates should encourage greater research and development, enterprise and innovation. All of this should boost long run economic growth. Governments over the last 15 years have been keen to close the unfavourable **productivity gap** between the UK and some of her major competitors such as France and the US (see Chapter 6).

● ● Knowledge and Application: Government spending

Figure 10.4: UK Government spending 2014-15 by area, £bn

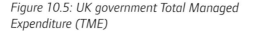

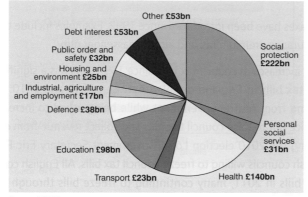

Source: HM Treasury

Figure 10.5: UK government Total Managed Expenditure (TME)

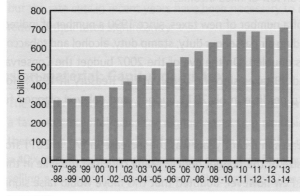

Source: OBR

Figure 10.6: TME as a % of GDP

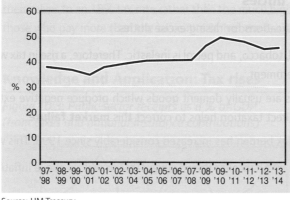

Source: HM Treasury

There are two types of government expenditure. **Current expenditure** is public sector spending on goods and services, such as medicines, and other types of recurring expenditure such as public sector salaries. **Capital expenditure** on the other hand, is investment in infrastructure such as motorways, railways, school and hospitals. Governments have been keen to boost capital spending since 1997, with major projects such as Cross-Rail, and the regeneration of the area surrounding the Olympic Park. The sum of these two types gives Total Managed Expenditure (TME), which reached £732bn in 2013-14.

Figure 10.4 shows that the biggest single area of expenditure is Social Protection, which includes Jobseekers Allowance, Employment and Support Allowance, state pensions and other social security benefits.

Analysis of government spending trends

The recession of the early 1990s caused the public finances to worsen significantly. The budget deficit reached 6.3% of GDP in 1993-94. The Labour government that came to power in 1997 pledged to be prudent in public expenditure, and avoid large budget deficits. In the first few years of office this objective was undoubtedly achieved. TME reached just 34.5% of GDP in 2000-01, compared to 43.0% in 1993-94.

From 2000 onwards, however, Labour increased public spending dramatically. Education, health, transport, housing, crime, and defence all received large increases in real terms expenditure. This spending boosted GDP growth significantly during the period, acting as a **Keynesian stimulus**. The 2002 Comprehensive Spending Review announced an annual average real increase in spending on health of 7.3%, and 5.7% on education, along with big boosts for other departments. Total expenditure on health rose from 7.0% of GDP in 2000 to 9.6% in 2010, finally surpassing the OECD average which the UK lagged behind for decades.

However, the 2008-09 recession caused the budget deficit to increase dramatically, and despite the Coalition government's pledge to protect NHS spending, most government departments have experienced real terms cuts since 2010 as part of their fiscal consolidation strategy.

Figure 10.7: UK spending on healthcare and education as a % of GDP

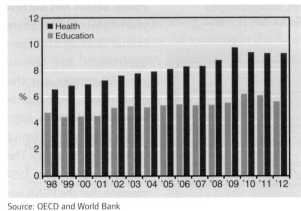

Source: OECD and World Bank

How beneficial were Chancellor Brown's spending increases?

There are several economic arguments supporting a rise in spending on the NHS. They are:

1. **Rising life expectancy** – The UK has an **ageing population**, who will require more medical care in their old age. Thus, more NHS spending is necessary to provide for their treatment.

2. **Productivity and labour force participation** – Better healthcare should reduce the number of people deemed to be unable to work due to health problems, thereby boosting participation rates and labour supply. Also, a healthier population should be more productive.

3. **Increasing expectations** – Higher standards of living has led to rising consumer expectations of the NHS.

4. **Technological advance** – As new and often expensive drugs and treatments have been discovered, people naturally want them. So new supply has created new demand.

5. **The crisis in the NHS** – By 1997 waiting lists for procedures were long and public spending on healthcare as a percentage of GDP was well below most of the UK's European neighbours.

There are several economic arguments supporting a rise in spending on education. They are:

1. **Productivity and competitiveness** – By improving attainment in education the workforce should become more productive, thus increasing supply side growth. As the UK has historically experienced an unfavourable productivity gap to her competitors, improving education is important. Furthermore, in a globalised world, the UK needs a skilled workforce to compete.

2. **Social mobility** – By 1997 many schools in poorer areas were underperforming and dubbed by the term 'sink schools'. By investing heavily in improving schools, particularly in poorer areas and through the academy program, greater equality of opportunity should result, thus improving social mobility, raising aspirations and reducing intergenerational poverty.

3. **Plugging skills gaps** – By the early 2000s there were skills shortages in many sectors which needed addressing.

● Evaluation: Have things improved?

With little doubt there has been a significant improvement in public sector healthcare and education provision since 2000, as well as improvements in other public services. Waiting lists are down, and educational attainment is up, spectacularly in some areas, such as London state schools. However, there is a serious question over how efficient public spending has been. A 2011 report by the ONS revealed that although public service labour input rose by around 15% between 2000 and 2008, labour productivity in the public sector actually fell during this period. In addition a measure of 'value added' public sector output growth lagged well behind the growth in public sector spending during this period, suggesting that higher funding was too often not translated into greater public service provision. A common criticism was that too much funding was used to hire administrative staff and managers, rather than on front line staff and services.

government, causing public debt to soar, as shown in Figure 10.9. In 2014 the Office for Budget Responsibility (OBR) predicted that public sector net debt would peak in 2015-16 at 78.7% of GDP, though many believe this is optimistic.

Evaluation: Has the government managed the public finances well?

During Labour's first term (1997-2001) they were fiscally prudent, and the public finances improved significantly, with public debt falling as shown in Figure 10.9. After the 2000-01 fiscal year government spending rose considerably. Several taxes were raised and introduced but this was not sufficient to prevent the emergence of repeated budget deficits during a time of strong growth in the mid-2000s. Although the

Figure 10.10: Total gross general government debt, Q1 2014, % of GDP

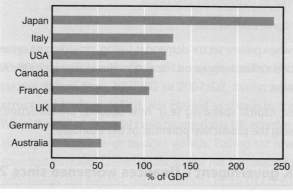

Source: OECD

causes of the severe 2008-09 recession were arguably out the government's control, going into that period running a structural budget deficit did not help, and the government's own fiscal rules had to be abandoned. Having compared favourably before the 2008-09 recession, public debt has risen to levels higher than some other OECD countries, as shown in Figure 10.10, though the Coalition government's policy of 'austerity' has improved the relative public debt standing of the UK somewhat.

Figure 10.11: Selected European ten-year government bond yields

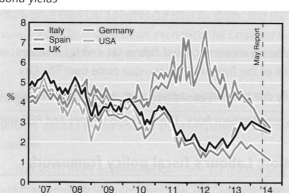

Source: Bank of England

Many in the Coalition Government who took office in 2010 were fearful that investors could become alarmed by the rate at which UK public debt was rising, and that they would insist on higher rates of interest on government bonds issued. The Coalition government presented a detailed and strong commitment to budget deficit reduction, through tax rises and departmental spending cuts. Although Labour have criticised the government for cutting 'too far, too fast' and choking off the recovery, the policy has seemed to quell investor fears, as the UK government has been able to borrow at very low rates of interest, as shown in Figure 10.11.

In part this has been due to investors fleeing from bond markets in struggling Eurozone economies such as Greece, Portugal, Italy and Spain, with bonds issued by the UK, Germany and the US being seen as relatively 'safe havens'. However, fears of default by the large Southern Eurozone economies of Italy and Spain have subsided, as shown by falling bond yields from mid-2012 in Figure 10.11.

● ● Application and Analysis: International comparison of public finances

The UK has traditionally been seen as a middle-to-low ranking country in terms of government spending as a proportion of GDP, embracing free markets more than many of her 'statist' European neighbours. However, Figure 10.12 shows that government spending as a percentage of GDP in the UK has moved close to the Eurozone average and has a 'middle' ranking. This provides further evidence of the Labour government's more interventionist approach. However, government spending remains considerably lower than countries with a strong social democratic tradition, particularly in Scandinavia. The Coalition's deficit reduction policy is set to reverse the trend seen under Labour, as significant public sector job and spending cuts, combined with a robust rise in private sector output and employment is set to continue reducing the public sector's share of GDP.

Figure 10.12: General government expenditures as a percentage of GDP (2012)

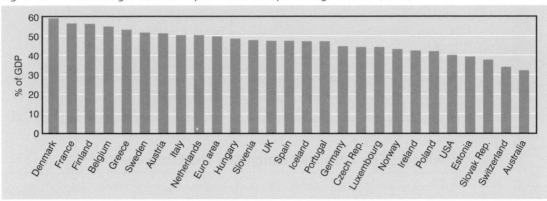

Source: OECD

Figure 10.13: Total tax revenue as a % of GDP (2012)

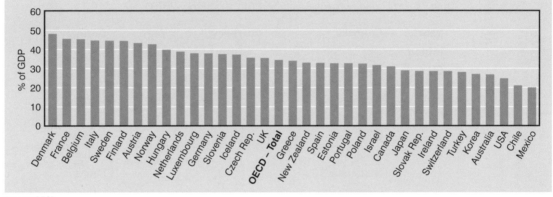

Source: OECD

Figure 10.13 shows that the UK is a middle ranking country in terms of tax revenues, with tax receipts as a percentage of GDP slightly higher than the OECD average in 2012. The UK has a higher tax burden than more free market economies such as the United States, but a lower tax burden than more interventionist North European countries. Although the UK does not have high relative tax rates, she does have a high degree of tax *compliance*, which pushes her up the tax revenue as a proportion of GDP rankings.

● ● Knowledge and Application: The impact of the Euro on fiscal policy

The EU Growth and Stability Pact (GSP), adopted in 1997 stated that countries joining the euro could not run budget deficits exceeding 3% of GDP, and national debt could not rise above 60% of GDP. Although the UK did not join the euro, Labour's fiscal rules followed a similar theme to those adopted by Eurozone countries, which aimed to stop Eurozone governments undermining monetary policy by adopting contrary fiscal policy measures. France and Germany were the first ones to break the GSP. Following this, many Eurozone counties broke the GSP, and on the eve of the global financial crisis in 2007 many Southern Eurozone countries like Italy, Greece and Portugal had accumulated national debt levels of around 100% of GDP. When the global recession of 2008-09 led to a significant worsening in the public finances in most Eurozone countries the GSP was effectively abandoned, like Labour's fiscal rules. By 2014 Eurozone countries were trying to carve out a new GSP, with greater scrutiny over national budgets by Brussels and harsher penalties for countries who break the rules, to ensure the Eurozone debt crisis is not repeated.

Chapter 11

The United Kingdom and Europe

This chapter will address the following key questions regarding the UK and Europe in 2015:

- What advantages and disadvantages arise from UK membership of the EU?

- What costs and benefits have arisen from EU enlargement?

- What advantages and disadvantages might arise from the UK entering into European Monetary Union (EMU) and replacing sterling with the euro as its currency?

- Given the economic crises in Europe since 2008, what might the future hold for the EU and the eurozone?

● Knowledge: **The European Union and the Eurozone**

The United Kingdom is one of the 28 members of the European Union. Table 11.1 shows how the European Union has evolved, from its initial existence as just a free trade area for coal and steel towards deeper and wider economic, social, political and even monetary union.

Table 11.1: EU and eurozone members (as of January 2013)

Year joined EU*	Country	Currency = euro	Year joined EU*	Country	Currency = euro
1952	France	*	2004	Cyprus	*
	Germany	*		Czech Republic	
	Italy	*		Estonia	*
	Belgium	*		Hungary	
	Netherlands	*		Latvia	
	Luxembourg	*		Lithuania	
1973	Denmark			Malta	*
	Ireland	*		Poland	
	United Kingdom			Slovakia	*
1981	Greece	*		Slovenia	*
1986	Portugal	*	2007	Bulgaria	
	Spain	*		Romania	
1995	Austria	*	2013	Croatia	
	Finland	*			
	Sweden				

*or equivalent at date of entry

The candidate countries for EU membership are currently Iceland, Montenegro, Serbia, FYR Macedonia and Turkey.

● Analysis: **What are the advantages of UK membership of the EU?**

The European Union is a **customs union** with free trade between members (freedom of trade in goods and services, freedom of movement of labour and capital) and common external tariffs imposed on imports from outside the EU; every member must set the same tariff (import tax) on imports of agreed goods and services.

The key microeconomic advantages of the **Single European Market (SEM)** are:

- EU members can specialise their production to create and deepen mutual gains from trade.

- The SEM creates European-wide competition, which should drive down costs of production, leading to…
  - Greater efficiency in EU firms
  - Opportunities for successful firms to enjoy economies of scale across Europe-wide markets
  - Lower prices and more choice for EU consumers
  - Greater incentives to invest, leading to dynamic efficiency gains

The key macroeconomic advantages of the SEM are:

- Productivity is raised due to increased efficiency and investment.

- Inflationary pressures are reduced across EU markets.

- Unemployment may fall as real wages rise and free movement of workers eases local labour market problems.

- GDP growth is encouraged.

The UK's Department of Business, Innovation and Skills estimate that EU members trade twice as much with each other as a result of the SEM. Over half of the UK's exports are sold to other EU countries. A European Commission study of the SEM in 2007 found that the SEM raised EU GDP by €233bn, adding 2.2% to GDP, and that 2.75 million jobs were created between the introduction of the single market in 1992 and 2006.

● Analysis: **What are the disadvantages of UK membership of the EU?**

Critics of UK membership of the EU (including the supporters of the United Kingdom Independence Party, or UKIP) point out the following issues with EU membership:

- Local and domestic unemployment resulting from UK firms either moving overseas or being competed out of existence by lower cost producers in the EU.

- Freedom of movement of labour has created competition in labour markets in countries such as the UK, where net migration has been inward.

- Increased immigration places pressure on public services, housing and infrastructure, particularly in regions where net immigration is particularly high.

- EU membership costs the UK over £6 bn per year.

- A significant portion of the EU budget is spent on the Common Agricultural Policy, which critics argue is inefficient, raises food prices, creates significant food waste and disproportionately benefits major agricultural producing members of the EU.

- As several EU countries have struggled to recover from the credit crisis and the recession which followed, there has been pressure on other EU members to contribute to 'bail-out' funds.

- Trade with other EU members has simply replaced trade which the UK used to conduct with other non-EU economies. **Trade creation** occurs when joining a customs union reduces the price of imported goods. **Trade diversion** occurs when joining a customs union increases the price of imported goods. In the latter case, it could be argued that when the UK joined the EU they were forced to buy more agricultural produce from within Europe, as the newly-imposed common external tariff priced non-EU trading partners such as Australia and New Zealand out of UK markets.

● Knowledge: **EU enlargement in practice**

The EU has grown from its original six members in 1952 and now forms an economic superpower with a population of over 500 million and a combined GDP of around £11 trillion (larger than the USA and Japan combined).

Chapter 12

The UK in the World Economy

This chapter examines the UK's position in the global economy, as well as the challenges and opportunities the UK economy is likely to face in the coming decades.

● Knowledge: **The UK and globalisation**

Globalisation is such a multi-faceted issue that it is hard to define precisely. Globalisation can be taken to mean the increasingly free flows of goods, services, capital, people, information and cultures around the world. Advocates of globalisation and free trade believe that countries will specialise in their area of **comparative advantage**. This is where one country can produce a good or service at a lower opportunity cost than another. Put simply, the theory implies that if each country specialises in producing the good or service they are relatively best at, resources will be allocated more efficiently, total global output should rise, and overall economic welfare will be improved. The NICE decade between 1997 and 2007 was a period of rapid globalisation.

● Analysis: **How has globalisation affected the UK economy?**

As shown in Figure 12.1, growth in global trade tends to rise more rapidly than world GDP growth, implying that imports and exports as a percentage of GDP have been rising in most countries, due to the increasingly free movement of goods and services. Figure 12.2 shows that between 1990 and 2013 global merchandise trade more than tripled, despite a fall in global trade during the 2008-09 global recession.

Figure 12.1: Growth in volume of world merchandise trade and GDP, 2005-15

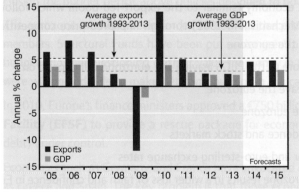

Source: WTO Secretariat

Figure 12.2: Volume of world merchandise exports, 1990-2015, Indices, 1990 = 100

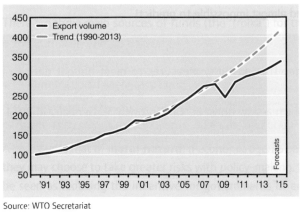

Source: WTO Secretariat

The UK economy is no exception, and has seen growing import and export volumes over the last two decades (see Chapter 5 for more detail). Imports and export values were close to 30% of GDP in 2012.

Figure 5.2 in Chapter 5 highlights the UK's move to specialise in the production of services, in which it is a large net exporter, at the expense of manufactured goods, in which the UK is now an enormous net importer. Over the past two decades, Newly Industrialised Countries (NICs) such as China and others in the Asian Pacific Rim have become able to produce manufactured goods at a much lower cost than producers in the UK and other Most Developed Countries (MDCs). At the same time the UK has a clear comparative advantage in the production of services due to the use of English as the international business language, a long standing reputation for excellence in professional services such as accounting, law and finance, and the existence of the City of London as the world's leading financial centre.

Figure 12.3: Manufacturing and financial services as a % of GDP

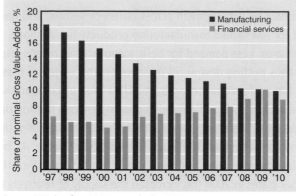

Source: ONS data from HM Treasury budget 2012

Figure 12.4: GDP and financial services output growth

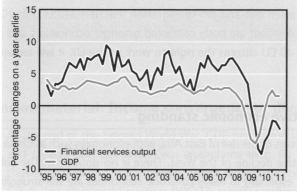

Source: Bank of England

Figure 12.5: Share of nominal GDP accounted for by financial services

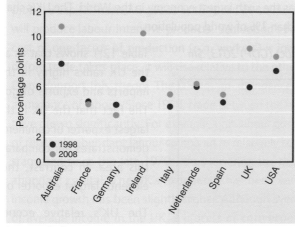

Source: Bank of England

Figure 12.3 shows that the manufacturing sector has shrunk considerably as a proportion of the UK output since 1997, while financial services have grown in importance. According to the ONS business services and finance accounted for 29.3% of GDP in 2012, with manufacturing accounting for just 10.3% of GDP, and just 8% of jobs in 2014. Since the 1980s the UK's relatively more relaxed attitude towards free markets has led to governments doing less to support manufacturing in the face of new competition from East Asia than many of her competitors such as France and Germany, and significant deindustrialisation occurred. The manufacturing sector's share of UK GDP fell to levels significantly lower than France and Germany. Areas of Southern Scotland, South Wales and Northern England have been particularly affected by industrial decline. Some of these areas remain blighted by high rates of unemployment and welfare dependency. While manufacturing has declined as a share of GDP, Figure 12.4 shows that in the decade leading up to the 2008 financial crisis, GDP growth averaged 3% per annum while financial services output averaged around 6%, increasing the sector's share of GDP considerably.

Figure 12.5 shows that financial services' share of UK GDP has risen considerably between 1998 and 2008 to levels far higher than in similar sized European economies such as France, Germany and Italy.

There are problems associated with being dependent on services and financial services in particular. Firstly services are more difficult to export than goods due to language barriers and regulation. The European Union, the destination for 50% of UK exports, has very effectively removed barriers to trade in goods, but have been much less successful in removing barriers to trade in services. Exporting services outside of the EU is even more difficult. As shown in Figure 5.2, the trade in services surplus does not match the trade in goods deficit, leading to a persistent overall trade deficit. The second problem is that there are risks associated with being dependent on finance and banking. Unlike other sectors, if banks get into trouble and go bust there are much wider implications for the economy. Households and firms will lose their savings; other banks will become much less willing to lend and business and consumer confidence will plummet. In 2007-08 some of the UK's biggest banks such as RBS and HBOS faced bankruptcy. The Labour government decided that the consequences of not bailing out these banking giants would be too great to risk, and spent billions of pounds saving them.

and achieve self-sustaining economic growth. To accumulate capital, economies must have reasonably high savings ratios, or bring in capital from overseas, through trade or access to finance from institutions such as the World Bank. Many economies in Sub-Saharan Africa are unable to accumulate sufficient capital. Poverty leads to low savings rates, primary product dependency leaves countries vulnerable to a worsening in the terms of trade, which means they can import less in exchange for their exports. In addition, some economists believe that LDCs must reach a certain 'social capacity' before they can take-off, through reducing problems such as corruption and health issues to a critical level that allows for self-sustaining growth to take place.

● Analysis: How would 'rebalancing' help the UK economy?

Switching from consumption and imports, to investment and exports

Since the financial crisis started in 2008, there has been a consensus amongst policymakers and economists that the UK economy has become too dependent on consumption (fuelled by excessive household borrowing) and imports. The Conservatives in particular also believe that the UK economy has become too dependent on government spending, funded by excessive public sector borrowing. The Bank of England and the Coalition government have both called for a 'rebalancing' of the economy away from consumption and imports, towards investment and exports. This should help to bring more balanced and sustainable growth. A consensus has also emerged that the UK economy has become too dependent on services, and the manufacturing base of the economy has shrunk too much. Therefore many believe that boosting the manufacturing sector's share of the economy should be part of the rebalancing process.

Despite the consensus that rebalancing would be beneficial, there have been few specific policy initiatives designed to help the rebalancing of the UK economy. After a 24% depreciation in 2008, the pound has settled at a lower value than during the NICE decade (1997-2007). This should help to improve net exports, but the weaker pound is not the result of deliberate government policy. One government initiative to boost 'green' investment is the founding of the **UK Green Investment Bank** in 2012. The plc aims to attract private funds to finance the private sector's investments related to environmental improvements. The **Funding for Lending Scheme (FLS)** set up jointly by the Treasury and the Bank of England in 2012 aims to boost investment by enabling banks to borrow at lower rates on the condition that they lend more to businesses and consumers. One criticism of quantitative easing (QE) is that much of the cash injection has been stuck in the financial system, with banks remaining unwilling to lend, and many small businesses complain about the lack of access to credit, which impedes investment. The FLS aims to address this, by increasing the amount of loans given to businesses, and thus increase investment.

Figure 12.7 shows that the government expects the share of GDP accounted for by consumption and government spending to shrink, the latter by some 4.5%, and the contribution of investment and net trade to grow as a share of GDP between 2011 and 2016. The fall in government consumption's share of GDP is mostly due to the Coalition's spending cuts in an attempt to reduce the size of the budget deficit.

Figure 12.7: OBR forecast change in shares of GDP 2011-16

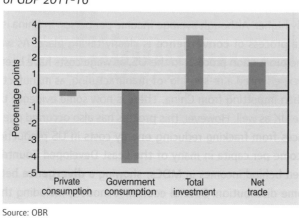

Source: OBR

Despite some glimmers of hope, by 2014 there was little evidence to suggest that significant rebalancing had taken place, either in terms of the components of GDP in Figure 12.7, or between the manufacturing and service sectors. According to the ONS, when the Coalition took office in the second quarter of 2010, manufacturing accounted for 10.7% of GDP, and business services and finance accounted for 28.8%. By 2013, manufacturing's share of the economy had shrunk to 10% of GDP, with manufacturing output 8.9% below its pre-crisis peak, while business services and finance output had grown to 32% of GDP. Exports of goods and services have increased since the depths of the 2008-09 recession, but so have imports, and there has been no significant improvement in the trade balance, and the trade in goods deficit is bigger than ever (see Chapter 5). Total managed expenditure (TME) by government was significantly higher in 2013-14 as a proportion of GDP (45.6%) than on the eve of the financial crisis in 2007-08 (40.8%), while private sector investment's share of GDP is lower than pre-crisis levels, at 15.1% of GDP in 2013 compared to 17.1% in 2008. If the shares of GDP in the UK economy do rebalance, it is likely to take some time.

● Analysis: **What can the UK do to boost net exports?**

Figure 12.8: Eurozone quarterly GDP growth rates (% quarter-on-quarter)

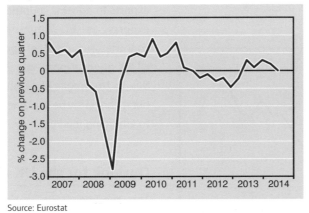

Source: Eurostat

Figure 12.9: Eurozone quarterly imports of goods ($bn)

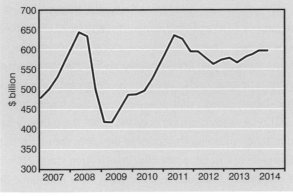

Source: OECD

Many countries in the Eurozone have been gripped by an ongoing debt crisis and uncertainty over the future of the currency union since the world economy went into recession in 2009. As a result growth in Eurozone economies remains very weak, and many euro area economies have slipped back into recession since 2009. Around 40% of the UK's exports go to Eurozone countries. Figures 12.8 and 12.9 show that weak GDP growth in the Eurozone has caused consumers to purchase fewer imports, thus causing Eurozone import growth to stagnate. This means there is little potential for a significant rise in demand for UK exports from Eurozone members, reducing the likelihood of an export-led recovery and a 'rebalancing' of the economy towards exports.

Faster-growing developing economies, on the other hand, provide a significant opportunity for export growth, and the Coalition government have been keen to boost trade relations with these countries. Since taking office in 2010 the Prime Minister David Cameron has visited several of these countries on trade missions, including Brazil, China and the UAE.

Germany has been very successful at growing exports, usually of hi-tech manufactures and capital goods, to the fast growing developing economies, the **BRIC**s in particular. German exports to China for example more than doubled between January 2007 and January 2012. The UK however, has so far been less successful at 're-orienting' trade towards these emerging markets, which is disappointing, but there is a clear opportunity for growth in this area. As well as trade deals, the stabilisation of the pound at below pre-financial crisis levels should help to make UK exports more competitive. Figure 12.10 shows that the pound has fallen in value, while the currencies of China and Brazil have risen significantly, which should help to boost UK exports to these emerging markets.

Despite not being as successful at re-orienting trade towards emerging markets compared to other advanced European economies, UK exports to both India and China rose by around 55% in the 5 year period after January 2007, and Figure 12.11 shows that by 2012, for the first time in decades, UK goods

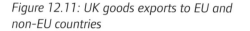

Figure 12.10: US dollar exchange rates, January 2005-March 2014, indices of US dollars per unit of national currency, 1 January 2005 = 100

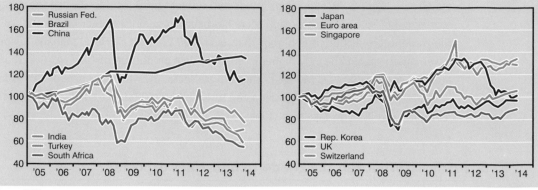

Source: WTO

Figure 12.11: UK goods exports to EU and non-EU countries

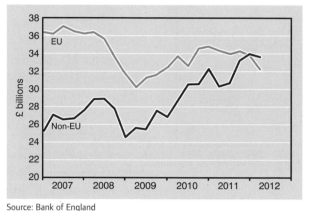

Source: Bank of England

exports to non-EU countries exceeded goods exports to EU countries, and non-EU countries accounted for approximately half of all UK goods exports into 2014. This is partly due to the fragile state of the EU economy, but it can partly be explained by rising exports to emerging markets.

Outlook for the UK economy

The medium term outlook for the UK economy is uncertain. Since the 2008-09 recession growth forecasts have proved highly inaccurate, frequently over-predicting growth between 2009 and 2012, but the pace of GDP and employment growth in 2013-14 took many by surprise when the recovery finally arrived in earnest. There are however, many who doubt the sustainability of the recovery. Firstly, many economists believe that the recovery so far has been based on increases in consumption due to a falling savings ratio and rapid house price growth, centred in London and the South-East. It is not the balanced, broad-based growth that policy-makers had hoped for. Secondly, despite a rapid increase in employment in 2013-14, many question how 'inclusive' the recovery has been, as nominal wage growth has lagged behind inflation meaning the squeeze on living standards has continued. There also remains the ever-present downside risk to UK economic growth from stagnation in the Eurozone. In 2014 France and Germany, the engines of the Euro area economy, saw economic growth stall. In the autumn of 2014 Euro area inflation fell to just 0.3% and the threat of a prolonged period of Japanese-style deflationary stagnation loomed large. This would impact negatively on the UK economy through lower exports, reduced business and consumer confidence, and a possible banking crisis in the event of sovereign credit defaults. In addition, growth in emerging markets such as Brazil and China has weakened, making a rebalancing of growth more difficult than ever. Finally, with the budget deficit and borrowing remaining stubbornly high, continued austerity measures will put downward pressure on growth. However, there are reasons for optimism. The educational attainment of the workforce is higher than ever, continued falls in unemployment resulting in higher wages should restore real wage growth, there are signs of rising business investment, and immigration is likely to add to the size of the labour force. Whether the robust growth experienced in 2013-14 is sustainable or otherwise, it is far more welcome than no growth at all. In the longer term however, the performance of the UK economy is likely to depend on whether a return of productivity growth can be achieved, combined with a rebalancing of the economy away from consumption and imports towards investment and exports.